Divine Dialogues

by

Rev. LaVonne Rae Andrews/Welsh

and

Dr. Don Welsh

DEDICATION

For our Children:

REV. LAVONNE'S
Reena, Larrin, Donelle and Brandyn

DR. DON'S
Laura, Julie, Jennifer and Marc

Introduction

These Divine Dialogues were the result of our authorship of a weekly column in The Paso Robles Press in which we shared our insights and ideas on various spiritual topics.

You'll notice that Rev. LaVonne's viewpoints frequently include a Native American slant and Dr. Don's include scriptural references.

We both present ideas stemming from our training as Ordained Ministers of the Centers for Spiritual Living, in which we share this practical and positive teaching and way of life. Nearly every column includes a quotation by the founder of this worldwide movement, Dr. Ernest Holmes, whose ideas are as valid today as when he wrote and spoke them in the first half of the 20th century.

The columns align with the 52 weeks; you can use them as a spiritual focus all year. Of course, you're welcome to read them in any order as determined by your own Infinite Wisdom.

Thank you to the members and friends of the Center for Spiritual Living in Templeton, California for supporting us in our many projects that led to connecting with the community of northern San Luis Obispo County in Central California. Also thanks to the editor of the Paso Press, Brian Williams, whose open mind and professional approach welcomed our broad philosophical leanings, and to Josh Petray, our original editor, who embraced and encouraged us.

We are knowing that these Divine Dialogues make a difference in advancing your spiritual understanding and that you are experiencing the resultant wholeness, abundance, creativity, wisdom, peace and love the you are meant to enjoy.

Rev. LaVonne and Dr. Don

Divine Dialogue #1
The One Mind

Dr. Don: No matter what name is given to the Universal Creator, Spirit, Father, God, Jehovah, Great Spirit, Allah, or the One Mind, the thing I am referring to is the Infinite Source of Life, Love, wisdom, abundance and peace.

Rev. LaVonne: This week we focus on the one Mind, your mind. The word Mind when capitalized represents the inter-connectedness of one and all through the wisdom of God.

Dr. Don: James Redfield, the author of the classic book, *The Celestine Prophesy*, notes, "All religion...is about humankind finding relationship to one higher source. And all religions speak of a perception of God within, a perception that fills us, makes us more than we were."

Rev. LaVonne: It's so freeing to know that there are many paths to the Divine and that even though all are unique, there is a path for each one. I know that you are divine and serve a special purpose on Mother Earth.

Dr. Don: Referring to the poet, Robert Browning's words, "All is love, yet all is law," Ernest Holmes, the founder of Religious Science, explained that these are two aspects of God. Love is the givingness of Spirit, and the law is the invisible energy field through which all creation takes place. It's the law of cause and effect.

Rev. LaVonne: It's through the law that all things are possible. To quote the Bible, "Is anything too hard for the Lord?" (Genesis 18:14) and, therefore, is anything too hard for you? With God at your core, I believe you can overcome any seeming challenge. You are more powerful than you know. Let God lead and watch your life change.

Dr. Don: This makes it possible for seeming miracles to manifest in your life.

Rev. LaVonne: In truth, all of life and all experiences on this planet and beyond are miraculous.

Dr. Don: I find it amazing that love and law work so consistently. You can even use them where it may not seem beneficial.

Rev. LaVonne: Can you give an example?

Dr. Don: Sure. There was a woman in front of me at the bank. In chatting, she mentioned she'd been fired from her job and was depositing an "unemployment" check. Evidently, the lady had grown weary of working and thought she wanted a change. She commented: "You've got to watch what you think." How true.

Rev. LaVonne: Yes, she was using the same creative law that ended up giving her what she thought she wanted. Imagine focusing on something positive that you'd like to experience in your life. Allow your Spiritual self to emerge. Let your divine Mind be free to respond to your inner Source.

Dr. Don: Holmes wrote, "God is in, through, around and for us." Choose what you'd like: love, prosperity, wellness, peace of mind and wisdom. Your life can be all you want it to be when you connect with the one Mind.

Both: And so it is.

Divine Dialogue #2
The Way the One Mind Works

Rev. LaVonne: Mind is God in action. And that's you and me.

Dr. Don: Since God is love and love is givingness, the Universal Mind gives all the goodness of life. When you have a need and ask to receive the answer, the Infinite potentiality has already provided it.

Rev. LaVonne: All you have to do is accept. And you accept it by seeing it, feeling it and entering into a state of gratitude. That is the blessing of your inborn Spirit.

Dr. Don: "You are indeed the light of the world." (Matthew 5:14) God gives you whatever is needed to express that light: abundance, joy, health, harmony, happiness, wisdom and total peace of mind. When you are being your true self, your inner light shines.

Rev. LaVonne: The beauty of being your true God-self is that you are a joy to be around and you attract others who are allowing their light to shine. I find it compelling to be in the presence of those who are like-minded.

Dr. Don: A Hindu story tells of the gods Shiva and Shakti, who are watching the earth. Looking down, they see a poor man walking along a road. Shakti is compassionate and convinces her husband, Shiva, to drop a bag of gold in front of the man. The man is so involved in his problems, trying to figure out where to get his next meal, that he steps over the bag. He thought it was a bag of rocks.

Rev. LaVonne: How often are you so caught up in your own challenges that you don't notice the blessings that God constantly gives?

Dr. Don: Ernest Holmes wrote, "It is entirely a question of our own receptivity."

Rev. LaVonne: It is a belief in the good or God within, that you know the right thing is morphing into place.

Dr. Don: Can you give an example?

Rev. LaVonne: Yes. Besides being a Minister, I'm a professional actress and often commute to Los Angeles to audition or perform. On the way to an audition I'm cognizant of my thinking process. In truth, I wouldn't drive three and a half hours if I thought I wouldn't get the role. So, I'm open to all legitimate possibilities and outcomes.

Dr. Don: If you find yourself blocking the gifts of God, there are some spiritual tools to help open your consciousness to receiving the good. Open your mind by sitting quietly, meditating on the qualities of the Divine. Say a positive affirmation such as "I am prosperous, healthy, loved and loving."

Rev. LaVonne: "To understand the immeasurable, the mind must be extraordinarily quiet, still." (Jiddu Krishnamurti)

Dr. Don: Another way to open to Spirit is to say an affirmative prayer giving thanks that God is already answering.

Rev. LaVonne: Allow God to work through you. It's your gift to the universe. This planet needs you.

Both: And so it is.

Divine Dialogue #3
What the Mind Does

Dr. Don: Seekers of Truth want to know the basic principles by which things work. We like to make sense of life. To do that, Rev. LaVonne and I have taken a positive and practical approach to determine the nature of the one Mind, the way it works and what it does.

Rev. LaVonne: You and I are seekers of Truth, God's Truth, the Truth of Spirit that dwells within. And the Mind, which is capitalized, is the Mind of God. That Mind also dwells within. That is why you, your God-self, recognizes the Truth. You can just feel it and know when it is right.

Dr. Don: What is this Universal Mind? What do you think of when describing God? I think of love, intelligence, nature's perfect pattern, the Source of infinite abundance, creativity, wholeness, joy, peace and the wisdom of life.

Rev. LaVonne: Whatever your description, it's yours to choose. What I know is that Spirit is always available, especially when you get your limited self out of the way. Ralph Waldo Emerson wrote, "Let us take our bloated nothingness out of the path of the divine circuits."

Dr. Don: So, what is your role in this relationship between God and you? Yes, you are made in God's image and likeness. Yes, you are a reflection of the divine Light. Yes, God's love always gives and gives. So, what's left? You are the recipient.

Rev. LaVonne: You get to accept the abundance of God's love, giving-ness and all the other qualities of Spirit. Ernest Holmes wrote, "How much of (the) Infinite good is ours? All of it. And how much of it may we have to use? As much of it as we can embody."

Dr. Don: Embodiment means to take into your body or your experiences to express Spirit. It's like filling a cup that is empty. You can make room to accept God in your life. Be open to receive. Let your consciousness take it all in. I think Jesus let himself embody the nature of God so much that people called him Lord.

Rev. LaVonne: When you admire others and see their highest qualities, you are also seeing your own potential and possibilities.

Dr. Don: Scripture says, "All things are possible to him who believes." (Mark 9:23) When you believe in the Power for good and let it work through you, letting go of negative or mediocre thoughts and attitudes, you inherit the blessings of life, allowing the good to flow through you.

Rev. LaVonne: It's already in process. The fact that you're reading this is evidence of your desire to acknowledge and live as your best and highest self.

Dr. Don: Relax. Since you are already a spiritual being, Spirit leads your quest. You are immersed in and surrounded by the infinite good. Take it, use it; you are a blessing.

Both: And so it is.

Divine Dialogue #4
How to Use Mind

Rev. LaVonne: When you get something new do you read the directions in how to use it? As a child, someone may have taught you to ride a bike or maybe you learned on your own. Your mind (uncapitalized) didn't come with directions. The Mind (capitalized) is the Mind of God and the directions are enclosed, ready to be exercised.

Dr. Don: The directions have been interpreted through scripture, philosophers, writers and spiritual teachers. The bottom line is "God has given us a power and we must use it." (American philosopher, Ernest Holmes)

Rev. LaVonne: You can choose not to use your power and many people make that choice. I love to watch happy little children play. They absolutely believe they can do anything and can hardly wait to grow up. A little believing child still dwells within you.

Dr. Don: You can learn a lot about life through many beliefs and pathways. It's important to apply what you have learned, to live life to its fullest.

Rev. LaVonne: When you use the principles of Truth, you can reap the rewards of love, joy, peace, wellness and abundance. It is your opportunity to express your unique Spiritual gifts.

Dr. Don: You can prove to yourself that the ideas you believe in actually work to give you a better life.

Rev. LaVonne: The proof is in the way your life expands and changes. "Your life changes the moment you make a new congruent and committed decision." (Anthony Robbins)

Dr. Don: To be congruent means to be in agreement or in harmony. When you are in alignment with God your spiritual goodness shines; there is a positive shift that blesses everyone.

Rev. LaVonne: The decision of your commitment is to be true to yourself which in turn honors your Spiritual self. The Mind of God is always wanting to be expressed and you are the perfect receptacle for that privilege.

Dr. Don: That explains why, as Job said, "You shall also decree a thing, and it shall be established for you, and the light shall shine upon your ways." (Job 22:28)

Rev. LaVonne: Even when you are seemingly having a bad day, God is in the midst of your challenges and ready to revive your lightness in life. The challenges may even be gifts to get you to open to other possibilities.

Dr. Don: How do you decree a thing? Begin by stilling your mind and meditate on the wonderful aspects or qualities of the Divine.

Rev. LaVonne: Use an affirmative prayer to focus your attention on what you would like to attract into your life.

Dr. Don: When you experience a sensation that what you desire is already a reality, express your gratitude, knowing you have set into motion an energy that creates it.

Rev. LaVonne: By doing this process, you tap into the Divine Mind. And that's how to use it.

Both: And so it is.

Divine Dialogue #5
What's It All About?

Dr. Don: I like to think of February as the month of love. When you look at any quality in life, love is the most prevalent characteristic regarding that condition.

Rev. LaVonne: When it comes to wellness, love is the healer.

Dr. Don: When you're focusing on prosperity, love is at the root of attracting abundance.

Rev. LaVonne: Ideally, every relationship has some level of love as its basis.

Dr. Don: Love is what it's all about.

Rev. LaVonne: So how do you get to a point of selfless love? It all starts with loving yourself. Maybe that sounds contradictory until you remember that love, real love, always starts with God.

Dr. Don: Poet Edwin Markham had a disagreement with a banker friend who defrauded him. Markham was all set to retire when he found out that he couldn't because of what the banker had done. At first, he was bitter and had writer's block. An inner voice spoke to him, telling him to forgive. He ended up writing these lines:

"He drew a circle that shut me out –
Heretic, rebel a thing to flout;
But love and I had the wit to win:
We drew a circle that took him in."

Rev. LaVonne: Can you imagine expanding your circle of love to include people who are challenging? There are basically four kinds of love which the Greeks termed Eros, Familial, Philadelphia and Agape.

Dr. Don: Eros is romantic love. It's the kind of love we see in movies and on television. It's the subject of most Valentine cards, novels, songs, poems, and soap operas.

Rev. LaVonne: Familial love is the affinity between family members - between mother and child, siblings, parents, grandparents and closeness with other relatives.

Dr. Don: Philadelphia is brotherly love. William Penn founded the city of the same name and envisioned a community where people had compassion and caring for one another.

Rev. LaVonne: Ernest Holmes wrote, "One of the first things to do is to love everybody. If you have not done this, begin to do so at once. There is always more good than bad in people, and seeing the good tends to bring it forth. Love is the grandest healing and drawing power on earth."

Dr. Don: Agape means spiritual love. It describes the deep caring between God-centered spiritual travelers. Divine relationships bring selfless love into your connections and communications.

Rev. LaVonne: How can you attract all these kinds of love to your life? Easy. Go back to the basics and know that God is love and love is God. Since God loves us all equally you have the ability to love in the same manner as God.

Dr. Don: Leviticus 19:18 advises, "Love your neighbor as yourself." The implication is that you first love yourself, then you can love others, the whole world and beyond. Yes, it's all about love.

Both: And so it is.

Divine Dialogue #6
Be My Valentine

Rev. LaVonne: Hearts, flowers, candy, red, pink and more, are ideas associated with Valentine's Day. For me, they represent love. All kinds of love, from romantic love to God's unfailing love.

Dr. Don: Everyone wants someone to love and to be loved. Usually, Valentine's Day denotes romantic love. Yet, love is love and when you have a high level of affinity for another, that could be your Valentine.

Rev. LaVonne: Since you are a Spiritual Being, to BE a Valentine is to be filled with the essence of love.

Dr. Don: Real love isn't about earning it. You don't have to be a certain way to be loved. This is unconditional love; accepting the other exactly the way they are and the way they are not.

Rev. LaVonne: That may seem like a tall order at times. When situations occur where someone seems to push your buttons, that's the time to refocus on your true self and allow your Spiritual self to show through.

Dr. Don: Recent research shows that across cultures, people tend to experience emotional sensations in similar ways. When they're angry, muscles tighten. When they feel love, there's a sensation of warmth.

Rev. LaVonne: You attract the attributes of who you are. "Life is a mirror and will reflect back to the thinker what he thinks into it." (Ernest Holmes)

Dr. Don: So when I request that you "Be my Valentine," I am asking you to share the essence of Valentine's Day with me and I with you. I am accepting you the way you are and you are not. I am also requesting the same from you. "A friend is someone who knows all about you and still loves you." (Elbert Hubbard)

Rev. LaVonne: 1 John 4:7 reads, "Dear friends, let us love one another, for love comes from God. Everyone who loves has been born of God and knows God." Even though you may doubt or question this, I believe that at your core, it is the truth about you.

Dr. Don: I have a suggestion for today or any day. Even if you don't have a special person you call "Valentine," how about giving someone flowers, candy, a thoughtful note or your undivided attention. See how it makes you feel.

Rev. LaVonne: It could even be a gift to someone you don't know, like opening a door or sending off your loving thoughts to other countries and nations. Love is a universal phenomenon.

Dr. Don: The Divine Love that is God, loves you unconditionally and is always sending you Valentine gifts. Spirit says, "Be my Valentine." The entire Bible book *The Song of Solomon,* speaks of this relationship between you and the Beloved.

Rev. LaVonne: So, be the love that you desire and see how every phase of your life expands lovingly. Think thoughts of love, especially when challenged; turn every situation toward love. It totally works.

Both: And so it is.

And the Rains Came

Dr. Don: After a long period of dry weather, some members of our Center asked if Rev. LaVonne could lead a rain dance, since she is Native American (Tlingit tribe, Raven clan).

Rev. LaVonne: At first I was hesitant, since for most tribes and nations, many of our dances are sacred and have significant meanings. And, it's not up to us to attempt to manipulate Spirit.

Dr. Don: When she realized the intention of setting a collective communal consciousness, recognizing the powerful Spiritual nature that dwells within everyone, Rev. LaVonne agreed to facilitate the gathering.

Rev. LaVonne: It was heartwarming to welcome so many beautiful spirits from near and far who deeply care about our planet Mother and the gifts from Father Sky.

Dr. Don: It was fun for a few of us guys to do the drumming; we ranged in age from eight to eighty-four.

Rev. LaVonne: The fellows were in the center of the circle and the drumming represents the heartbeat of Mother Earth.

Dr. Don: It's important to open every ceremony with a prayer, thanking all our relations and the Creator for all our blessings. Rev. LaVonne also sang a traditional Navajo song expressing love and joy.

Rev. LaVonne: The participants and the Templeton Park attendees learned the Round Dance which uses a traditional, simple dance step and is part of nearly every Powwow.

Dr. Don: Watching the dancers circling around me and feeling the energy of the other drummers as we provided the heartbeat gave me a deep sense of love, awe and belonging.

Rev. LaVonne: The truth is, Spirit knows exactly what it is doing and Mother Earth and Father Sky comply.

Dr. Don: The intention was not to make something happen; instead, to express gratitude.

Rev. LaVonne: "The natives showed us extraordinary kindness; for because of the rain that had set in and because of the cold, they kindled a fire and received us all." (Acts 28:2)

Dr. Don: The coming together of so many people of diverse beliefs and backgrounds for a common cause was a blessing beyond words.

Rev. LaVonne: The kindred spirit that reigned with the synergistic circle, set the scene for the rain that splattered the earth the next morning.

Dr. Don: Some wanted to give Rev. LaVonne the credit. Others speculated that it was a coincidence.

Rev. LaVonne: I know that every individualized Spiritual Being has the consciousness to create miracles.

Dr. Don: The next day, as we were gathered for our Sunday Celebration and explained the joy of the rain dance, it began to rain!

Rev. LaVonne: Some laughed, some cried tears of joy and a few of us went outside and welcomed the moisture with upraised arms, smiles and gratitude.

Dr. Don: Here is a quote that says it all. "Anyone who thinks that sunshine is pure happiness, has never danced in the rain." (Anonymous)

Both: And so it is.

Divine Dialogue #8
An Aye for An Aye

Dr. Don: The story is told that Jesus disagreed with some old scripture verses. He knew people had heard "an eye for and eye, a tooth for a tooth." He advised his followers that it is not about getting even, but about forgiveness or turning the other cheek.

Rev. LaVonne: As I see it, when you turn the other cheek, you are seeing things from a new perspective which leads to a different viewpoint.

Dr. Don: There is a law of cause and effect, that assures that what you give out returns in like kind. This law always agrees with your ideas, statements, actions, thoughts and words. It says "aye." You get an aye for an aye.

Rev. LaVonne: So how are you currently living your life? Is it good, full of abundance and love? Are you happy? Are you living your potential? Are you allowing your true spiritual essence to be expressed?

Dr. Don: Your life experiences are created out of what you've already accepted into your subconscious mind, which is the seat of this law of cause and effect. Joseph Murphy in *The Power of Your Subconscious Mind* wrote, "Over 90% of your mental life is subconscious, so men and women who fail to make use of this marvelous power live within very narrow limits."

Rev. LaVonne: So what happens if you're feeling self-limited or not feeling full of Spirit? Sometimes you may need a little reminder of your greatness. The other day I noticed a sign in a restaurant which had the heading: "Today's Special." Underneath someone had chalked in: "So is tomorrow."

Dr. Don: Your attitude about life determines how you'll experience it. If you think it's going to be a fantastic, joyful, fulfilling day, it is. But if you've concluded that life is hard, that everything's against you, or that you'll never get ahead, it becomes a self-fulfilling prophecy.

Rev. LaVonne: Recently, I was staying at a campground near Los Angeles while in rehearsal for a play at the Autry Museum. As a researching actress, I love listening to conversations. Some are exhilarating and some are heart-wrenching. The differences are in how the speaker reacts to various situations in their life.

Dr. Don: Sometimes a person's identity gets invested in self-limiting beliefs. Your ego is your human identity and people can get stuck in ego. There is also a higher identity, your Divine self, the truth of your being. To move beyond self-limitation into the acceptance of greater good, you can shift the focus from ego to the Divine.

Rev. LaVonne: You also have the Divine connection to use your insight and send living, loving thoughts to others, including strangers and help enlighten their lives. It feels good to send out your light, which is God's light. Sometimes I've been instantly rewarded by a radiant smile.

Both: And so it is.

Divine Dialogue #9
Let Go and Let God

Rev. LaVonne: There's a popular saying: "Let go and let God." Imagine how uncomplicated your life can be by implementing that simple affirmation.

Dr. Don: As we approach what's known as Lent, do you wonder its significance? It's a time churches identify as the forty days leading up to Easter. Some traditions demonstrate personal belief and faith during Lent by giving up something.

Rev. LaVonne: Is giving something up a sacrifice?

Dr. Don: There may be some value in using this time as an opportunity to assess one's habits and choices and in using the power of intention to set change into motion. However, would a loving God want you to deprive yourself of life's many blessings by limiting your good?

Rev. LaVonne: The challenge of allowing my mind to express personal decisions is appealing. Knowing that Spirit is in the center of my Being, reminds me to use this internal gift in positive and loving ways.

Dr. Don: Jesus advised "When you fast, do not look sad like the hypocrites; for they disfigure their faces, so that it may appear to men that they are fasting." (Matthew 16:6)

Rev. LaVonne: When you are able to give up the feeling of attachment to all things and see life through the perspective of Spirit, blessings abound. Recently, I performed in a World Premiere play in Los Angeles. The playwright was brilliant in releasing her attachment as she worked with the actors, director, producers and crew. As a result, her efforts became a synergistic, fulfilling and rewarding experience.

Dr. Don: How about giving up alternative attachments for Lent? I'm sure you wouldn't miss fasting from doubt, negativity, fear, control, perfectionism or manipulation.

Rev. LaVonne: "We must let go of the life we planned, so as to accept the one that's waiting for us." (Joseph Campbell)

Dr. Don: You could also use this season to look forward to the renewal and rebirth that's celebrated with the coming of Spring.

Rev. LaVonne: Seasons happen on their own accord by way of Spirit. You don't have to try to make the seasons change. You don't have to stand over a flower demanding it to bloom.

Dr. Don: The word flower already contains a "flow." Just let go and let the life-force flow freely everywhere, in nature and in yourself. The divine law already has infinite creative power and it blossoms on its own.

Rev. LaVonne: Spirit wants to be expressed and automatically springs forth.

Dr. Don: Ernest Holmes wrote, "A steadfast determination to attain some purpose, the letting go of all that opposes it, a complete reliance upon the law of good, and an unqualified trust in Spirit - this is true fasting and real prayer."

Rev. LaVonne: Why not let this season be an opportunity to reveal more of that natural spiritual nature that is within you.

Dr. Don: Let go and let God.

Both: And so it is.

Divine Dialogue #10
Dealing with Anger

Dr. Don: Research reveals reasons to avoid getting angry. Yet, this powerful emotion can be used productively and transformed in healthy ways. Unexpressed anger holds dangers by itself.

Rev. LaVonne: It is reported that anger can cause stress, high blood pressure, heart trouble and pre-mature aging. And yet, angry mothers started the organization MADD (Mothers Against Drunk Driving) that has demonstrated a beneficial influence on society.

Dr. Don: It seems the key to handling anger is to seek a balance in moderating its expression.

Rev. LaVonne: So where does anger come from and does everyone harbor anger somewhere in their lives? Psychologically, anger can be a healthy emotion since it's a defense mechanism and a survival instinct.

Dr. Don: Scripture provides much wisdom concerning anger. "A soft word turns away wrath; but a harsh word stirs up anger." (Proverb 15:5)

Rev. LaVonne: That quote makes me think of my mother who also had a soft voice. One of my favorite Bible verses is: "A fool gives full vent to his anger, but a wise man keeps himself under control." (Proverb 29:11)

Dr. Don: Set against these multiple admonishments to avoid expressing anger, John 2:13-17 contains the vivid description of Jesus seemingly losing his temper in the Temple. He actually took a whip and drove out the moneychangers. When is righteous anger meant to be expressed?

Rev. LaVonne: I trust that's a rhetorical question. In the past I've used anger to move me forward, to get a job done or accomplish something. Since God gave us an ability to express all emotions, methinks that anger can be used productively.

Dr. Don: Ernest Holmes acknowledges "...degenerative thoughts can be turned into creative, energizing, vitalizing ones. Anger can be turned into love, and the very power that has been destroying can be made to build up..."

Rev. LaVonne: So how do you deal with anger? Do you stuff it, explode, cry, hit a pillow or take it out on some innocent bystander?

Dr. Don: You could breathe. Deepak Chopra, M.D. points out that anger constricts the blood flow and when the brain isn't getting blood, you aren't thinking clearly. So he suggests controlling the breath like you do when meditating. Slow, rhythmic breathing helps restore emotional control.

Rev. LaVonne: It's also been proven that regular exercise is beneficial in preventing angry outbursts. If all of the above is too time consuming, just do the tried and true...count to ten.

Dr. Don: You have the God-given ability to choose your emotions. You can make a conscious choice to avoid expressing anger toward someone, including yourself.

Rev. LaVonne: To me, love is always the answer when there's a choice to make. Leo Buscaglia wrote: "Don't hold to anger, hurt or pain. They steal your energy and keep you from love."

Dr. Don: And a final thought, "Do not let the sun go down upon your anger." (Ephesians 4:26)

Both: And so it is.

Divine Dialogue #11
Drink Living Water

Rev. LaVonne: "If you only knew the gift God has for you and who you are speaking to, you would ask me, and I would give you living water." (John 4:10)

Dr. Don: This advice from Jesus was spoken to a woman at a well. The water he was talking about wasn't really water at all, it was the Christ-like nature. The well is a metaphor for the spiritual nature at our very depths. You can find the Source within yourself.

Rev. LaVonne: The Source is Spirit. Spirit is God in action. You and I are a part of the Divine plan. Spirit is expressed by and through all sentient Beings. How blessed it is to know this Truth.

Dr. Don: I think everybody thirsts for that spiritual connection. It's commonly said that people who drink too much alcohol are really thirsting for God. Therefore, they look for Spirit in a bottle.

Rev. LaVonne: In truth, Spirit dwells within. It saddens me when I recognize a non-believer of knowing there is a higher power. In our Native American culture we see the Great Spirit in all people and things, equally.

Dr. Don: If people don't feel that Presence, they might feel that something is missing in their life and try to compensate through other methods of fulfillment. Empty space is not to be confused with nature abhorring a vacuum.

Rev. LaVonne: Nature has already filled you with all that is needed to lead a fulfilling, purposeful life. When you step out of the way of your true self, Spirit provides wisdom, understanding, compassion and all the qualities of God that reside within.

Dr. Don: Ernest Holmes wrote, "We should hold out the cup of acceptance until it is filled and overflowing with the manifestations of our desires. This chalice of the heart is held up that the heavenly flow may fill it with God's abundant life."

Rev. LaVonne: It may mean that you start with a tiny cup of acceptance. Maybe it's just the size of a thimble. Once you get into the habit of accepting the generosity of Spirit watch your life change in positive ways. Then move on to a bigger container so you can share your abundance with others.

Dr. Don: I think people frequently forget to hold out the cup at all. It's seemingly a fast paced life and time tends to get filled with busyness. Getting involved with work, schedules, and distractions like television, the Internet and family obligations, compromises your self-love moments. Just make time to go to the well for living waters.

Rev. LaVonne: God doesn't force the issue or interfere in your life. You get to take the first step. You have every resource to accomplish all desired inspirations.

Dr. Don: Once you begin quenching your thirst, relax and allow your mind to drift, meditate, listening to the Divine Word of Spirit. It's there, especially for you.

Both: And so it is.

Divine Dialogue #12
Your Eternal Nature

Dr. Don: I noticed the centuries old oak tree next to our Center is showing new life. The tips of the branches are tinged with green. Every year for hundreds of years, it has come back to life, resurrected from the apparent "death" of winter.

Rev. LaVonne: Spring is here and now it is time for rebirth and renewal.

Dr. Don: Everything is coming to life again. The hills are green, flowers are blossoming and our back yard Wedding Garden is ready for the Spring activities.

Rev. LaVonne: Life is expressing. Springtime gives us an opportunity to more fully understand the amazing phenomenon of the ongoing nature of life and our eternal nature.

Dr. Don: Master teacher, Jesus, provided the perfect example that reveals the true nature of humankind.

Rev. LaVonne: "We are spiritual beings having a human experience." (Pierre Teilhard de Chardin)

Dr. Don: It is a section of a continuous journey of an eternal life we all are having. Ernest Holmes wrote, "Let us learn to view eternity as a continuity of time, forever and ever expanding, until time as we now experience it shall be no more. Realizing this, we shall see in everyone a budding spirit, a becoming God, an unfolding soul, an eternal destiny."

Rev. LaVonne: This is a perfect opportunity for us to see one another as divine creatures of the most high. In my Native American roots, we honor all beings and things of nature as spiritual. Nature gives us an opportunity to witness the ongoing-ness of God, knowing that the spirit lives on, even as it appears to have died.

Dr. Don: So what does that mean to us right now? I think it means we might as well be happy, enjoy every moment of life and be grateful that God is so good.

Rev. LaVonne: Great Spirit gives life and experiences that live through all of creation.

Dr. Don: That not only includes all of nature and this magnificent universe, but also you and me. "I have come that they might have life and have it abundantly." (John 10:10)

Rev. LaVonne: We are not only deserving of abundance, but worthy to enjoy all of God's blessings. Now is the perfect time to focus on our freedom, well-being and God's abundance. We celebrate the peace of Spirit.

Dr. Don: Peace prevails when we no longer have worries or concerns about what happens at the end of our earthly experience. What happens is sublime, blissful, joyous and amazing. This is a time to celebrate. Celebrate the lives of loved ones whose memories you cherish. Celebrate the wonderful expressions of nature. Feel the oneness of your spirit with the Divine. Remember who you are.

Rev. LaVonne: Life is eternal and so are you. Take heart in this awareness. Love the Life that lives as you, and be lifted up to celebrate Springtime.

Both: And so it is.

Divine Dialogue #13
Life is a Song

Dr. Don: Just like a bird, you are destined to sing. I believe you are meant to be happy, loved and loving, healthy and whole, prosperous and fulfilled.

Rev. LaVonne: Sounds easy doesn't it? And, in truth it is. Spirit needs to be expressed and singing is one way to feed the desires of God.

Dr. Don: There are some birds that don't sing; they twitter. And while that's the way God created them, they sing or twitter automatically.

Rev. LaVonne: I wonder if that's how the social media network got the name *Twitter*.

Dr. Don: Humans make choices. You can choose to go with the flow of the divine and express your spirituality or you can block your blessings by choosing to be a victim of problems, limitations, sicknesses or belligerences.

Rev. LaVonne: Of course, you could just twitter. For a bird that's making little chirping sounds which is how some people sing. It doesn't matter the notes or sounds, it's the expression of Spirit that makes a difference. A formula for your song might be: "Sometimes B sharp, never B flat, always B natural."

Dr. Don: There may be an urge within you that is pushing toward your greatness. You may feel like singing, but unless you cooperate with that urge, the music may be blocked.

Rev. LaVonne: A friend of ours who felt musically challenged said: "I must have a lot of music in me because it never came out."

Dr. Don: "I will pray with my Spirit and I will pray with my understanding also. I will sing with my Spirit and I will sing with my understanding, also." (I Corinthians 14:15) Understanding implies your ability to make a conscious choice to let the divine nature within you live life to its fullest.

Rev. LaVonne: When you live in cooperation with your natural divine flow and follow your dreams, it's a fantastic way to instill your God-filled desires.

Dr. Don: Ernest Holmes, who synthesized ancient wisdom into a philosophy and way of life wrote, "We may stumble, but always there is that Eternal Voice, forever whispering within our ear, that thing which causes the eternal quest, that thing which forever sings and sings."

Rev. LaVonne: How do you learn to "sing and sing?" When you pray affirmatively, meditate on the blessings of life, focus on the power, beauty, love and joy you can see everywhere, your life is a song.

Dr. Don: It begins with a decision: either tune in to the Mind of God or revert to old limitations.

Rev. LaVonne: Just like a car, you can use the same power to go forward or in reverse.

Dr. Don: Nicholas Sparks wrote: "Life, he realized was much like a song. In the beginning there is mystery, in the end there is confirmation, but it's in the middle where all the emotion resides to make the whole thing worthwhile."

Both: And so it is.

Divine Dialogue #14
The Divine Urge

Dr. Don: You don't have to be a fortuneteller to predict your future.

Rev. LaVonne: When I first heard the term, the Divine Urge, it was as if my purpose in life suddenly became clear. It explained why I was lead, driven and enthusiastic about the path my life was taking.

Dr. Don: There is something within, that beckons a Spiritual connection. It may come as an intuitive awareness, an emotional yearning or even a physical sensation. It's that "still, small voice" that whispers a spiritual invitation.

Rev. LaVonne: Our movement's founder, Dr. Ernest Holmes, referred to that inner impulse to push outward as the Divine Urge. I agree. It's an inner desire to express life.

Dr. Don: Scripture claims, "For the creation waits with eager longing for the revealing of the sons of God." (Romans 8:19) The Creator desires that we seek and discover the Presence.

Rev LaVonne: To know our presence is the ideal. Several years ago I was blessed to attend a gathering where Thich Nhat Hanh was the speaker. He wrote: "The most precious gift we can offer is our presence. When mindfulness embraces those we love, they will bloom like flowers."

Dr. Don: Even when a flower blooms or a plant grows, it is the one Life responding to the Divine Urge for full expression. Every time you do what comes naturally, you are expressing your true spiritual nature. And it feels good and right.

Rev. LaVonne: And goodness is the perfect response to Godliness. In truth you are a manifestation of God's perfection. How good it is to know this truth and allow yourself to be set free from self-doubt, fears or anything else that is unlike your perfect Spirit.

Dr. Don: Ancient wisdom reflects these same truths. In about 600 BCE, Lao Tzu, the old master of Taoism, said, "As rivers have their source in some far off fountain, so the human spirit has its source. To find this fountain of spirit is to learn the secret of heaven and earth."

Rev. LaVonne: The beauty is you don't have to take a long trek around the world and study for years to find the secret of heaven on earth. Why? Because it's right now, right this second, within you.

Dr. Don: One immediate way to experience this connection is through meditation. While the goal of meditation may be relaxation or mindfulness, for me the goal is to feel at one with a Higher Power and repeat "I Am One with the Infinite."

Rev. LaVonne: By being in alignment with your authentic self, a sense of tranquility and peace is available. The bonus that I have experienced, when I'm dialed in to that centeredness, is that others of like-mind seem to automatically appear in my life.

Dr. Don: Attracting these folks may seem like a coincidence; to me it merely reflects something going on at a deeper level. It's the Divine Urge in action.

Both: And so it is.

Divine Dialogue #15
Take the High Road

Dr. Don: Whether you realize it or not, you and I are on a Spiritual path. No matter what religion or faith orientation you follow, if you're seeking the Truth, you'll likely live in a higher state of consciousness. This is the high road.

Rev. LaVonne: Several years ago while training to be a Minister in L.A., I was assisting the Senior Minister on the pulpit. As we were waiting in the back of the sanctuary, we noticed a tough looking motorcyclist with what is considered an obnoxious word on the back of his leather jacket. The Minister quietly said to himself: "Take the high road."

Dr. Don: Ernest Holmes wrote, "An evolved soul judges no one, condemns no one, but realizes that all are on the road of experience, seeking the same goal, and that each must ultimately find his home in heaven."

Rev. LaVonne: Indeed, taking the high road may seem difficult at first, yet by remembering to respond to challenging situations positively, the path becomes easier.

Dr. Don: You might want to take a walk and enjoy the plants and flowers as they express God's beauty. By approaching life through gratitude and appreciation, I find joyful and empowering moments constantly.

Rev. LaVonne: Another way to accomplish a positive way of thinking is to develop a sense of humor. Studies indicate that humor is a learned response. So if you were never taught to see the lightheartedness of life, why not give it a chance? Joy is God-like.

Dr. Don: Sometimes in the midst of challenges, your may forget the reality of the goodness in life. Maybe you've been struggling with finances, relationship issues or health challenges. Yet, the truth of your being is abundance, love and wholeness; the way life is meant to be.

Rev. LaVonne: Anais Nin wrote: "We don't see things as they are, we see them as we are."

Dr. Don: Behind every challenge is the answer. Divine Intelligence is always providing opportunities to return life to a natural state of goodness. All the power of the universe is present right now to heal, provide, encourage and to love you. As your consciousness enters that place of peace within, Spirit always cheers you on.

Rev. LaVonne: God is the perfect cheerleader. I believe that God always wants the best for you and me. When you are in the midst of a seemingly tough situation, just allow your Spiritual Truth to show. Your mantra or cheer could be: "God is all there is and so AM I."

Dr. Don: As it says in Luke 3:5, "...let the crooked places be made straight and the rough places like a plain..."

Rev. LaVonne: Why not let God help straighten your path and join the high road to spiritual joy. As someone wrote: "Always take the high road...sometimes it will be a one way street but you're never going the wrong way."

Both: And so it is.

Divine Dialogue #16
Destiny's Journey

Rev. LaVonne: Everyone is on some kind of path. Whether it's occupational, social, Spiritual or trails in between, we are all on Mother Earth carving out our ways.

Dr. Don: The path that was carved by Jesus, including his entry into Jerusalem, was a Spiritual journey that gives us a great example of someone who took 100% responsibility for his life to which his self-chosen destiny led.

Rev. LaVonne: William Shakespeare said, "It is not in the stars to hold our destiny but in ourselves."

Dr. Don: Do you have a sense of purpose in your life? And are you following the journey of its unfoldment?

Rev. LaVonne: I believe that each one of us has a deep longing, a God-given desire, to fulfill.

Dr. Don: When we access inner guidance, an intuitive knowingness reveals the highest personal path that provides a sense of satisfaction.

Rev. LaVonne: The truth of your being wants to be expressed and Spirit is always available to answer the need.

Dr. Don: We experience a deep inner peace when we're on the right track. In fact, the meaning of the Hebrew word Jerusalem is: a place of peace.

Rev LaVonne: You are meant to be at peace, to live a full life and enjoy the process. Ernest Holmes wrote, "The universe must exist for the self-expression of God and the delight of God."

Dr. Don: The whole universe encourages you when you are doing what you are meant to do and to be.

Rev. LaVonne: That is a perfect example of the Law of Attraction. We attract to us, situations and people of like-mindedness who support our wants, dreams and desires.

Dr. Don: What if you feel you haven't accomplished your desires and dreams? What then?

Rev. LaVonne: There is no beginning or end on the Spiritual Path. Spirit is ready for you NOW, whoever, however, or wherever you are. In a sense, your destiny is now. As Lao Tzu is quoted, "A journey of a thousand miles must begin with a single step."

Dr. Don: A way to access your Spiritual nature when you feel stuck is to get quiet and listen to that inner voice that already wants and knows what's best for you.

Rev. LaVonne: Basically, it boils down to your consciousness. This life-giving energy is one of the many gifts of Spirit.

Dr. Don: There are many techniques that heighten consciousness.

Rev. LaVonne: Meditation, journaling, visualization, visioning...

Dr. Don: ...prayer-treatment, affirmations and more are all ways to leading a joyously fulfilling life.

Rev. LaVonne: When you are open to recognizing your highest Spiritual vibration, your life truly gets better and better.

Dr. Don: You know you're on your path of Divine destiny when it feels right and you can say, "I was born for this!"

Both: And so it is.

Divine Dialogue #17
The Upward Spiral

Rev. LaVonne: When I think of life as a whole picture, I'm comforted by these words of Ernest Holmes: "The spiral of life is upward. Evolution carries us forward, not backward."

Dr. Don: To me there are four R's of Easter: Rebirth, Renewal, Reunion, and Rising. The hills around our area are beginning to show the beauty of wild flowers of various colors. They are perennials, meaning they come back year after year which is a rebirth.

Rev. LaVonne: New life reveals the renewal of many kinds. Even the Easter bunny giving out eggs may represent the bounty of life, and it's a fun tradition of abundant fertility.

Dr. Don: Reunion is about reconnecting with Spirit. In *Find and use Your Inner Power,* metaphysician Emmet Fox wrote, "Easter if it has any true significance for us, must mean just this - that the winter of separation and limitation is over. It must mean that now we know who we really are - children of God - and what our real destiny is - reunion with Him."

Rev. LaVonne: Rising may refer to the proclamation, "He is risen." It can symbolize rising up out of our negativity; being positive.

Dr. Don: The upward spiral is different from a downward spiral in that rather than deteriorating, there's a germination of growth.

Rev. LaVonne: You and I have an opportunity to expand our consciousness beyond any seeming limitation (including death) when we remember to include God in the mix.

Dr. Don: I believe there are many dimensions of life and that we continuously move into higher levels. In the words of the Christ, "In my Father's house are many rooms; if it were not so, I would have told you. I go to prepare a place for you." (John 14:2)

Rev. LaVonne: Having had a near-death experience several years ago, I am convinced of a hereafter. That experience infused my current life in every way. It was as if Spirit gave me a chance to re-evaluate everything and everyone; it renewed my appreciation in a myriad of ways.

Dr. Don: The expanding light of consciousness allows Spirit to express through you too in a more loving, compassionate and supporting manner.

Rev. LaVonne: Recently, my husband and I took a short trip to Carmel to visit long time friends. When we traveled the roads I drove, while owning a business there, he asked if I'd ever gotten to the point of taking the scenery for granted. The answer was "never." In fact, sometimes I would remind myself: "Always remember this precious moment."

Dr. Don: Living in gratitude is a way to escalate that upward spiral.

Rev. LaVonne: I like a quote that came from the Monterey Bay Holistic Alliance: "It's not happiness that brings us gratitude, it's gratitude that brings us happiness."

Dr. Don: You have the chance right this moment to evolve ever upwardly on this magnificent Mother Earth. Just say "thanks!" Enjoy the process.

Both: And so it is.

Prayer is Not a Checklist

Rev. LaVonne: We like to pray before our meals. Recently, when Dr. Don said the breakfast blessing he included obligations we expected to do that day.

Dr. Don: With a twinkle in her eye, instead of saying "And so it is" or "Amen," she commented, "Prayer is not a check list."

Rev. LaVonne: We both laughed and that became today's topic.

Dr. Don: So, what is prayer?

Rev. LaVonne: To me, it's focusing my energy on an entity greater than me, called God, by allowing the power of Spirit to guide my life.

Dr. Don: I also focus on a feeling of the Presence of the Divine within me, and the loving qualities and characteristics of Spirit. Then, I sense my oneness with God and know that these qualities are also to some degree, within me.

Rev. LaVonne: "Prayer is the raising of one's mind and heart to God." (St. John Damascene) It's important to know that all thoughts are fed by Spirit and that it's your choice as to how you respond to this input.

Dr. Don: It's natural to turn to a higher Power when something seems absent in your life. I trust God to provide for my needs, wants and desires, or to remove something I no longer want. So, I look at what seems to be missing. However, the truth is that everything that makes life worthwhile already exists at the heart of my being. I possess God's gifts at some level.

Rev. LaVonne: Søren Kierkegaard wrote, "The function of prayer is not to influence God, but rather to change the nature of the one who prays."

Dr. Don: My prayer time is spent convincing myself that the Divine goodness is mine right now. Since God is already complete, then so am I. Spirit always loves, so nothing is withheld.

Rev. LaVonne: When you remember to remember the essence of the goodness of God, life becomes easier, happier and blessed.

Dr. Don: Effective prayers start with love. When praying for yourself, love yourself. When praying for another, love them. Love whatever challenge you want changed by releasing any negativity about it. "When we love, our prayers are answered and the gift of heaven is made." (Ernest Holmes)

Rev. LaVonne: There's a story about a Native American elder who was visiting a family in the city. Before supper, the family bent their heads and folded their hands to say grace. The Native elder asked what they were doing. The man of the house told him, it was their custom to express thanks for the meal...and didn't he pray before meals? The elder responded, "We pray without ceasing."

Dr. Don: Actually, every thought is a prayer.

Rev. LaVonne: So, in a way that is a checklist, noting all the things for which we're grateful.

Dr. Don: Why not take this moment to pray?

Both: And so it is.

Filled with Faith

Rev. LaVonne: Have you ever had a moment or a day when you just felt empty? I have. Then I learned how to become fulfilled!

Dr. Don: How did you do that?

Rev. LaVonne: Easy. I let Spirit in!

Dr. Don: How?

Rev. LaVonne: By allowing my innate faith to lead the way.

Dr. Don: What is faith?

Rev. LaVonne: It's a belief in some power greater than you. I call it the great I Am or God. How about you?

Dr. Don: To me, faith means aligning your thinking and beliefs with the Divine.

Rev. LaVonne: I like this quote by Ernest Holmes. "The faith *of* God is very different from a faith *in* God. The faith OF God IS God, and somewhere along the line of our spiritual evolution this transition will gradually take place, where we shall cease having a faith IN and shall have the faith OF."

Dr. Don: When I have faith IN God, I think of a power outside myself that may or may not grant my prayers. But when I have the faith OF God, I am intending that God's highest good is already mine and it is the Spirit within me that sets into motion the desired result.

Rev. LaVonne: Can you give me an example of that?

Dr. Don: Sure. If I'm experiencing a less than optimal level of wellness, I remember the perfect health that is the divine intention and I proclaim: "God's wholeness now expresses in, through and as me. I am healthy. Every cell is well."

Rev. LaVonne: And I know that works. In fact, I absolutely know that as your prayer is answered, it even builds more faith.

Dr. Don: Since every word you speak tends to be reproduced in your world, every word is powerful, even the negative ones. Be sure you aren't having faith in statements like "I don't feel well" or "I don't know what to do."

Rev. LaVonne: You want to make sure your words are backed by your highest intentions. For example, when I decided to move to Hollywood to be a professional actor, I first took it to prayer. Then I released the outcome because I had faith that Spirit would guide my path.

Dr. Don: The Creator is still rewarding you by providing the fulfillment of acting opportunities. The Invisible is still working through your agent and others to bring you auditions and parts you never could have imagined you would be given. As Paul wrote, "Now faith is the substance of things hoped for, the evidence of things not seen." (Hebrews 11:1)

Rev. LaVonne: When you live your beliefs, you truly are able to turn your world around, paraphrasing Henry David Thoreau. Knowing how to do this leads to a very fulfilling way of living.

Dr. Don: Affirm to yourself: Using the faith of God, I accept my highest good.

Both: And so it is.

Mother Earth: A Celebration

Rev. LaVonne: Mothers Day, and Native American Sunday share a common purpose in honoring Mother.

Dr. Don: The ideal Mother gives love, nurturing, wisdom, peace, joy and gives birth to each of us. The ultimate mother is the Earth. We all came from Mother Nature in union with Father Spirit.

Rev. LaVonne: When you live in alignment with nature you are experiencing the giving-ness of Spirit through the environment.

Dr. Don: Just as I loved my mother, so I love our planetary home and the perfect design of the celestial bodies and the Universe. The designer is Divine Spirit, which has given us the responsibility to take care of the planet, or as the Native Americans say, "be the caretakers of the land."

Rev. LaVonne: My father was born to the Tlingit tribe (Raven clan) in Wrangell, Alaska. I was blessed to learn from birth the value of this earth. "We were put here for a reason, to take care of this land. Not because it's something that maybe you say you own...but because it belongs to the next generation." (Rex Buck Jr., Wanapum tribe)

Dr. Don: In fact, the Native Americans say they take care of the land for the seventh generation. As I calculate, that would be over two hundred years, and that exceeds my expectation of this lifespan. So, if you do something for the seventh generation, you're doing it for offspring you will never see or know. You're doing it out of love, then.

Rev. LaVonne: And love is the answer to everything. God is love. You are empowered when you remember that the gift of God's love can change the world.

Dr. Don: As a Spiritual Being, you are always connected to God's love. When you express that love, you are duplicating the divine nature just like a good mother. This is the primary characteristic of female energy, which gives balance and blesses everyone in the world.

Rev. LaVonne: Quoting Lorraine Canoe, of the Mohawk tribe, "Everything that gives birth is female. When men begin to understand the relationships of the universe that women have always known, the world will begin to change for the better."

Dr. Don: This change is being birthed right now, just in time for a celebration of mothers and Mother Earth.

Both: And so it is.

Divine Dialogue #21
Three Spiritual Steps

Rev. LaVonne: It's more than "positive thinking," It's a WAY of thinking. Basically, it's "change your thinking, change your life" a description made by American philosopher Ernest Holmes.

Dr. Don: You have access to a Creative Force that is all-powerful, all-knowing, all-loving and everywhere present.

Rev. LaVonne: It's called God, or for some of us Native Americans: Great Spirit.

Dr. Don: Whatever word or phrase you name It, that feels right and works for you, is fine to use.

Rev. LaVonne: So, what are the 3-Spiritual Steps?

Dr. Don: The Creative Process involves:

>   Acknowledging the Power,

>   Aligning with it and

>   Affirming the blessings of Spirit.

The three A's.

Rev. LaVonne: This process truly changes your life. For example, a member of our Center wanted to sell their home, buy some property and build a new abode.

Dr. Don: Using the Creative Process, the member learned that the Source provides the wisdom and the way.

Rev. LaVonne: Part of the process is getting out of our own way and allowing Spirit (or Source) to work through us.

Dr. Don: Turn within, connect with this Higher Power and know that your desire is already accomplished.

Rev. LaVonne: How? Because Spirit gives you the idea in the first place!

Dr. Don: Out of the knowing that Spirit is supporting your inner desires you are free to experience greater gratitude and joy.

Rev. LaVonne: It's important to take action and cooperate with the outer world, attracting to yourself the right people, right situations and right action allowing the process to actually work.

Dr. Don: What was the result of that member using the Creative Process?

Rev. LaVonne: The house sold, the ideal property was obtained, the construction completed, and they're now living in their new home!

Dr. Don: And that's how the Creative Process works.

Rev. LaVonne: I believe the Creator always wants you to experience happiness, health, abundance of every kind, wonderful relationships and tons of love.

Dr. Don: After all, God is Love.

Rev. LaVonne: When you are aware of God's love, you experience even more love in your own life. The formula is really simple.

Dr. Don: It is using the three A's: acknowledging, aligning and affirming.

Rev. LaVonne: Spirit constantly gives and gives and gives, since God sees you as a perfect Spiritual Being made in the image and likeness of Itself.

Dr. Don: You are a being of light shining through the challenges of life.

Rev. LaVonne: When you remember that light, it eases the way.

Dr. Don: It's a partnership. God is already available. It's up to you to do your part and be all that you're meant to be.

Rev. LaVonne: And, it's fun. Once this formula clicks in, it becomes easier and easier to accomplish.

Dr. Don: Ernest Holmes loved to say: "There is a power for good in the universe, greater than you are, and you can use it."

Both: And so it is.

Divine Dialogue #22
Giving Thanks for Givers

Rev. LaVonne: The world is full of givers in many capacities.

Dr. Don: On Memorial Day weekend we celebrate those who have passed on after giving of their lives in so many ways. Memorial Day honors heroes of all kinds.

Rev. LaVonne: I feel that being generous is an inborn trait, that Spirit has given you an abundance of heart that transcends all self-imposed limitations.

Dr. Don: You may have learned that generosity sets you up to be taken advantage of. Yet, generosity actually attracts an abundance of good. It's a reciprocal universe. As you give, you receive.

Rev. LaVonne: In Corinthians 9:7 it says, "Each one must give as he has decided in his heart, not reluctantly or under compulsion, for God loves a cheerful giver."

Dr. Don: Everyone has something to give. No one else can give what you are uniquely qualified to give. You are the gift.

Rev. LaVonne: Recently, I read an inscription from a cemetery headstone in Ireland. It read, "Death leaves a heartache no one can heal, love leaves a memory no one can steal."

Dr. Don: One of my memories is about my deceased Dad who served on a Navy ship during World War II and carved replicas of it for my brother and me, which he brought home when he was on leave.

Rev. LaVonne: The term, "fight for our country" can be lovingly re-expressed when we remember that these men and women "gave for our country."

Dr. Don: I'm grateful that my Dad served, and even more, I appreciate the many gifts I received from him such as his humor, wisdom, intelligence and sense of practical spirituality.

Rev. LaVonne: Ernest Holmes wrote: "The universe must exist for the self-expression of God and the delight of God."

Dr. Don: Of course, as a part of the universe, your very existence pleases the Divine. You are so loved just the way you are.

Rev LaVonne: How great it is to know that when you are living your passion and truth, it is blessed by the wisdom of Spirit.

Dr. Don: The memories of the givers in our lives fill me with a sense of joy and gladness. What love they showed. Holmes pointed out, "Love is the central flame of the universe, nay, the very fire itself."

Rev. LaVonne: As you continue to bless all those who are no longer on the planet in living form, may you honor those who are alive and still a part of Mother Earth.

Dr. Don: Remember also, the gift that you are and as you celebrate the Holiday weekend, find ways to be a giver. We honor you.

Rev. LaVonne: "The National Day of Remembrance" is meant to help remind Americans of the true meaning of Memorial Day.

Dr. Don: On that day, why not pause at 3:00 pm to observe and honor these heroes in your own way.

Rev. LaVonne: May we pray together while giving thanks for the givers.

Both: And so it is.

What's Your Talent?

Rev. LaVonne: In a book discussion at the Morro Bay Library, one of the attendees asked about a character in the book: "What's her talent?" That question prompted this column.

Dr. Don: In scripture, Jesus tells a parable of the talents in which a man went on a journey and entrusted different amounts to three different servants. The one who received five talents traded and doubled the amount, the one who had gotten two, also invested it so he earned another two. But the servant who received one talent hid it, fearing he might make his master angry if he lost it, and gave back only one. (Matthew 25:14-30) A talent was the largest unit of weight in Biblical times and usually was used to measure gold or silver.

Rev. LaVonne: When I first learned this years ago, it impressed me since I translated that meaning to describe the value of our God-given talents. The dictionary defines talent as a natural ability or skill or a person possessing such an aptitude or skill.

Dr. Don: In interpreting the story of the talents, I think it could refer to aptitudes and skills. Those who use their God-given talents, receive abundantly. Those who, out of fear, hide their talents, often experience lack and scarcity.

Rev. LaVonne: Erma Bombeck wrote, "When I stand before God at the end of my life, I would hope that I would not have a single bit of talent left, and could say, 'I used everything you gave me.'" In truth we all have many talents, the trick is to use these gifts. And some people are still in the dark as to what their talents may be.

Dr. Don: Albert Einstein modestly claimed, "I have no special talent. I am only passionately curious." Whether you think of it as talent or not, each one of us is a unique Spiritual Being with multiple gifts and abilities given by the Creator.

Rev. LaVonne: When I was a Casting Director in Hollywood, I was amazed and impressed at some of the gifted and talented actors. When it came to placing them in film, television or commercial parts, talent had little to do with their getting the job.

Dr. Don: What then was their talent?

Rev. LaVonne: The director was often searching for a "look", a "type" or would say: "I'll know them when I see them." I soon learned it was an "energy" that got them the role.

Dr. Don: And that energy, I call God.

Rev. LaVonne: When you allow God to guide, to lead the way, all else falls into place. It takes trust, belief and faith to release our attachment to the results.

Dr. Don: So, what is your talent?

Rev. LaVonne: Just listen to that inner God Voice, the one that knows you better than anyone else.

Dr. Don: Just step aside and let God lead your way.

Both: And so it is!

The Apparent Parent

Rev. LaVonne: The word "father" often connotes emotional connections. It may be the Our Father, our Dad of origin or a substitute father image.

Dr. Don: We can reason that anyone who ever lived had a biological father and may have also had someone who functioned as a father figure.

Rev. LaVonne: In the Bible in John 14:10 it says "the Father that dwelleth in me, he doeth the works." Which means to me, that you have the availability of God's wisdom within and can even parent yourself.

Dr. Don: It seems the attributes of fatherhood are power, love, intelligence, wisdom, will or intentionality and action. Sensing these attributes in God, we tend to equate God's nature to our fathers.

Rev. LaVonne: Recognizing our divinity, we know we are spiritually connected to the Father.

Dr. Don: Jesus felt so close to his Father that he called him Abba, which could be translated using such an endearing word as Papa or Daddy. This closeness is expressed in John 10:30 as "I and my Father are one."

Rev. LaVonne: The Presence of God could be inferred by seeing the appearances that point to God:
- the beauty of the universe, our planet and environment,
- the amazingly creative ways that life shows up,
- the abundance of blessings,
- the delightful manifestations of love, joy and more.

Dr. Don: The effectiveness of prayer can be inferred by witnessing the ways apparent miracles show up, proving that the power for good can be relied upon constantly.

Rev. LaVonne: Yes, God is in constant support of your individualized expressions of your Spiritual energy.

Dr. Don: Why not use this Father's Day to remind yourself of the qualities of the Great Spirit, to honor your family fathers, and to empower yourself in tapping into the inner Father-Mother God being all that you are meant to be.

Rev. LaVonne: I love this quote by Ernest Holmes. "You are to recognize that you are already whole, perfect and complete in essence and that you have the capacity to be whole, perfect and complete in manifestation regardless of what may be appearing as a relative condition. And it doesn't matter how serious the condition is. There is no big or small in divine Mind be it a planet or a peanut."

Dr. Don: I am filled with gratitude when I recall all the wisdom and empowerment that my Dad gave me. I stand in awe when realizing the ways the Father continually blesses.

Rev. LaVonne: My Native American Indian father taught his seven children the importance of being loving and honoring the abundance of nature.

Dr. Don: It is an honor to be a father and even though my family is reared and living elsewhere, my intention is to live up to all the word father implies, even now.

Rev. LaVonne: Victor Hugo wrote: "We see past time in a telescope and present time in a microscope. Hence the apparent enormities of the present."

Both: And so it is.

Healthy Mind, Healthy Body

Dr. Don: Everybody wants to feel good physically, emotionally and mentally and the secret is to feel good from a Spiritual perspective.

Rev. LaVonne: When you can get your inner and outer thoughts in alignment with Spirit, your life can only get better in every way.

Dr. Don: The thing is, the Grand Design is perfect health. We are meant to experience wellness, vitality, aliveness and wholeness.

Rev. LaVonne: The reason? Because, God dwells within everything so we each have the capacity to replicate the perfection of Spirit.

Dr. Don: So why do people get sick? What causes them to feel badly?

Rev. LaVonne: When you forget to love yourself and others, you suffer consequences. Dr. Deepak Chopra, the author of many healing books tells us that the biochemistry of our bodies is the product of our beliefs, thoughts and emotions.

Dr. Don: There may also be negative or false beliefs that get in the way of wellness. When I hear "the flu is going around," I immediately think, "It's not going around me." And it doesn't.

Rev. LaVonne: This is why we have to remember to love ourselves. In the book *How to Find God in Everything,* Amoda Maa Jeevan writes: "Every unloving thought we have towards another or towards our self gets imprinted as a cellular memory that creates biological disharmony."

Dr. Don: We are in the Presence of Love, and knowing this automatically melts any false beliefs; we remove the self imposed barriers to perfection and experience the joy of perfect body, perfect mind, perfect soul.

Rev. LaVonne: A long practiced technique is meditation. When you allow yourself to empty your mind of all thoughts, negative and positive and just "be" you begin to feel the perfect Presence of Spirit that always dwells within.

Dr. Don: There are also other techniques that can get you back to your true spiritual nature of love and wholeness: affirmations and Spiritual Mind Treatment (positive prayer.) When you affirm, *I am whole, complete and perfect* or *Love heals me now*, you can trigger that memory of who you really are and be lifted to your normal, natural, healthy self. Love heals.

Rev. LaVonne: Ernest Holmes wrote in a Spiritual Mind Treatment: "I realign myself with peace, love, and joy and bring these qualities to my interactions with others." By using this seemingly simple formula you can change your life.

Dr. Don: Jeremiah 30:17 points out that healing comes from Spirit: "For I will restore health unto thee."

Rev. LaVonne: And since I know that you already are a perfect manifestation in the Mind of God, it makes total sense that any temporary diversion from your Truth is restored with Spirit.

Dr. Don: Divine Love does the healing. That Divine Love is within, around and moving through you in every moment. You are living in perfect health right now.

Both: And so it is.

Divine Dialogue #26
The Garden of Spirit

Rev. LaVonne: Great Spirit is all around you, everywhere. Most importantly it dwells within you.

Dr. Don: When I think of gardens, I think of God. In the words of George Bernard Shaw, "The best place to seek God is in a garden." The book of Genesis, starts out with a story of creation and goes right to humans living in a garden of beauty, peace and joy existing within.

Rev. LaVonne: In my Native American culture we tell the story of the "Three Sisters" (corn, beans and squash) who work together in germinating a garden. All three are planted in the same mound and work together so one plant helps nurture the other.

- Corn provides a natural pole for bean vines to climb.
- Beans fix nitrogen on their roots, improving the overall fertility of the plot by providing nitrogen to the following year's corn.
- The bean roots also stabilize the corn plants, they're less vulnerable to blowing over in the wind.
- Squash are shallow-rooted and become mulch, improving crops' chances of survival in dry years.
- Squash discourages predators from approaching the corn and beans.

Corn, beans and squash also complement each other nutritionally.

- Corn provides carbohydrates,
- Beans are rich in protein,
- Squash yields both vitamins (from the squash) and oil (from the seeds).

Dr. Don: In the garden, where all of Divine Nature's gifts are provided, it is a paradise. Human beings complete the picture by being able to appreciate the garden and are given the talent and intelligence to choose what to plant and how the garden can look in the future.

Rev. LaVonne: It would be interesting to plant a "Bible Garden" which would include any of the 125 plants that are mentioned in the Bible. Would all these species flourish where you live? Just like people we all seem to need various forms of nurturing to experience an abundant life. What I know for sure is that when God is your Master Gardener your life is truly enhanced.

Dr. Don: The Garden of Eden includes the Tree of Life that could symbolize the One Life that gives and gives, the One God. Then, there's the Tree of the Knowledge of good and evil, which is about choice.

Rev. LaVonne: I imagine that the Great Spirit, the Master Gardener, God, gave us Mother Earth to care for and nurture. It is a gift and we have the opportunity to choose how to be good caretakers of the land that we have inherited.

Dr. Don: When we were given dominion, it didn't make it okay to ravage the land or even to put up "no trespassing" signs. Dominion means good stewardship. Let the highest idea in the Mind of God guide every choice so that you are wise in your use of resources and let the beauty of the earth live beyond your lifespan, even beyond the seventh generation.

Rev. LaVonne: Having dominion does include choosing abundance over poverty, love over fear, health over sickness, peace over war and empowerment over victim-hood.

Dr. Don: We begin with an idea, vision, or intention for these preferences to be revealed in our garden. Choosing the best is up to you. There's a law of cause and effect operating all the time to act upon the choices you make. Then, the garden grows the choices automatically.

Rev. LaVonne: The seed is the highest idea, the soil is the law and the plants are the outer world results.

Dr. Don: With God, all things are plant-able!

Both: And so it is.

Divine Dialogue #27
Thy Will Be Done

Dr. Don: Do you resist the idea of a Power greater than you giving you instruction and guidance? Does your mind question "Whose will, will be done?"

Rev. LaVonne: As a child I wondered what "Thy will be done" really meant. A Sunday School teacher suggested that God always provides the highest and best direction in your life. At the time, I thought God was some old man in the sky. Now, I know that the perfect God is in, through, around and as, everything and everyone.

Dr. Don: Spirit is the Divine nature within you and me. So, when I say, "Thy will be done," it really means "My Divine Self knows." Ernest Holmes notes, "The intellect argues, but the Spirit knows."

Rev. LaVonne: Can we convince someone else into believing the way we do? I think not. In fact, Benjamin Franklin is credited with saying, "A man convinced against his will, is of the same opinion still."

Dr. Don: We admire a strong-minded independent thinker, yet the frame of mind needed to let "Thy will be done," is more like that of a child. Jesus taught that we must become as little children to enter the kingdom (consciousness) of heaven (peaceful state of mind.)

Rev. LaVonne: Yes. And your childlike mind wants to explore, invent and create. Then as adults we seem to want to cling to what we think we already know. In truth Spirit is never ending, allowing you to expand continuously and bless the world in return.

Dr. Don: After turning it over to the Divine, saying "Thy will be done," you may receive a thought, idea, or image that gives you a vision of how the particular blessing from Spirit is showing up. Then, as you continue to focus on that vision or thought, you are adding to the creative energy that operates to manifest it in the outer world.

Rev. LaVonne: And it is Spirit who is really behind it all. When you cooperate with your Divine Essence, life automatically becomes easier because Spirit wants you to be fulfilled.

Dr. Don: It's like a child asking the parent for something. You know the parent loves the child and wants to give. This is the "doing" part of "Thy will be done." Your job is to keep your attention on the vision. The Creative Mind will do the rest. In an ideal family, the child wants to receive and the parent wants to give.

Rev. LaVonne: And since we are perfect children of the most high, the "will" is an automatic meshing of mind, soul, Spirit and body.

Dr. Don: You can let your mind align with the Divine, allowing your soul to be one with Spirit and your body to harmonize with Nature. Ernest Holmes writes, "The Will of Life has only to BE Life."

Rev. LaVonne: Such simple words with powerful results: "Thy will be done."

Both: And so it is.

Divine Dialogue #28
What is the Truth?

Dr. Don: We've all heard about the truth. John 8:32 asserts, "And you will know the truth, and that very truth will make you free."

Rev. LaVonne: Those words have always perplexed me. I wondered what they meant. Was it what I learned as a child, to always tell the truth, or is it something greater? The musical *The Scottsboro Boys* includes a powerful song titled, "Make Friends With the Truth."

Dr. Don: You have the ability to separate the truth from facts. For example, a fact may be that you think you cannot afford something, but the truth is that you are abundantly blessed with unlimited prosperity possibilities.

Rev. LaVonne: Even scientific experiments rely on skepticism to be fully experienced and those facts too may change in time.

Dr. Don: Conditions always change. Relationships change. Your body changes. Maybe, even your understanding of how life works changes as you expand in knowing more of the truth.

Rev. LaVonne: Here is a quote by an unknown author: "People can't change the truth, but the truth can change people." God never changes. It's wonderful to know that there is a Presence that can be depended upon.

Dr. Don: The subconscious mind takes everything in, even things that are not the truth. That's where you come in. You can filter out those things that don't serve you, that are not the truth and return to Spirit.

Rev. LaVonne: Even thinking something like, "I'm sick and tired..." cements into the subconscious mind. That's when you can re-word that thought and tell your subconscious the truth by saying, "I am fully alive and filled with enthusiasm."

Dr. Don: American philosopher, Ernest Holmes, wrote, "We must test all ideas to see whether they are of the Truth. It is a mistake to accept every man's philosophy simply because it sounds plausible. We are to be on guard against accepting that which is not true. And let us remember this: the truth is simple, direct and always self-evident."

Rev. LaVonne: The real test of truth is to tap into how it feels to yourself; what resonates to you. Since God dwells everywhere, including within, let your Inner Wisdom be your guide.

Dr. Don: Since the one Spirit always wants the highest and best for you, the thought may be: "If this is really the Truth, does it feel as if it is of the Source? Would a loving God be the author of this?"

Rev. LaVonne: Mohandas Gandhi wrote, "Truth is by nature self-evident. As soon as you remove the cobwebs of ignorance that surround it, it shines clear."

Dr. Don: The inner spirit of wholeness, or Holy Spirit, awaits your recognition to see the light of Truth.

Rev. LaVonne: Spirit wants to be expressed through all of nature, including human beings. It's freeing when you realize that you're a Spiritual Being having a human experience. Now that's the truth.

Both: And so it is.

Divine Dialogue #29
Joyful Self-Expression

Dr. Don: Everyone wants to be happy and express joy in life.

Rev. LaVonne: And I believe since Spirit is at the center of our Being, we all can access that inner glow of glory.

Dr. Don: Yes, God is the source of joy and gladness. I like to say we believe in a God of Joy.

Rev. LaVonne: The Bible states in Psalm 51:8, "Make me to hear joy and gladness..." In *Discover a Richer Life*, Ernest Holmes wrote, "Life is not just something to be endured. It is to be lived in joy, in a fullness without limit."

Dr. Don: How can you find joy when you hear reports of violence, unfairness, poverty, or cruelty between people?

Rev. LaVonne: Since I know that we can always learn and expand using our Spiritual truths, I choose not to respond to negative experiences. To me, there is more joy than sorrow in life, especially when you focus on the positive.

Dr. Don: In his book, *Live & Love Fearlessly*, motivational teacher Bill Poett defines joy as "experiencing peace, gratitude, happiness, and contentment simultaneously."

Rev. LaVonne: And yes, this is possible. The way to do this is to trust Spirit, saying something like, "God is all there is, and so am I."

Dr. Don: When you are conscious of the goodness in life and dwell on the highest and greatest good, there is a law of cause and effect that reproduces your predominant feelings and you experience that greatest good.

Rev. LaVonne: The only thing that could get in the way is your own belief system. Joseph Campbell said: "Find a place inside where there's joy, and the joy will burn out the pain."

Dr. Don: When you eliminate any negative beliefs based on past experiences, your mind is ready to receive the best outcomes.

Rev. LaVonne: When you see a child deep in play or someone who is being creative, that is God in action.

Dr. Don: Set your intention for a joyous day upon waking and keep your attention on that image of joy in your mind. As you do that, you are supported by the tendency for good to happen, which overcomes any negatives, because the Divine Light replaces darkness instantly.

Rev. LaVonne: If your day seems to darken at times and your desire is to "have a good day" then put a smile on your face, fool your brain and allow your light to shine. Sometimes you need to coax yourself into a joyful expression.

Dr. Don: We're not talking about just having fun or joking around, but connecting with that deep reservoir of joy that comes from the spiritual realization of how blessed you are and how meaningful life can be. Out of this realization comes true joy.

Rev. LaVonne: So silence the doubts and make a joyful noise.

Both: And so it is.

Divine Dialogue #30
And So It Is

Dr. Don: Each week we end our column with, "And so it is." You may wonder what those words mean.

Rev. LaVonne: It's our way of saying "amen" a declaration of what was said before. The Hebrew Bible translates "amen" to mean "so be it." Some references claim it to mean "verily," "sealed in faithfulness" or "I tell you the truth."

Dr. Don: When we end a prayer, we have come to the point of knowing Spirit is clearly aware of our highest desires and intentions for the particular good for which we are praying. We have connected with the Divine and now know the good is ours. Gratitude completes the necessary ingredients of effective prayer. You can release any further concern by saying "and so it is."

Rev. LaVonne: Sometimes it's challenging to release our attachment to our prayer and let God lead us in the right direction. Even though we are inspired by Spirit and want to act upon these ideas, we get more mileage from the Divine when we just let go and let God.

Dr. Don: Ernest Holmes wrote, "Prayer is a thought, a belief, a feeling, arising within the mind of the one praying."

Rev. LaVonne: Whether you pray or not in a conscious manner, Spirit always wants the best for you. After all, you are an expression of God that can only be demonstrated through the personage of you.

Dr. Don: You can agree with God's gifts to you. "And so it is" becomes a confirmation of that agreement, much as two people may come to an understanding between them of some business arrangement or contract. Next time a serendipitous occurrence takes place, you could accept the seeming coincidence by saying "and so it is."

Rev. LaVonne: I love the quote by Audrey Hepburn: "Nothing is impossible, the word itself says 'I'm possible'!"

Dr. Don: I like that! After all, all things are possible to God and you are made of God-stuff. You are the hands and feet, the voice and individualized mind of the Creator.

Rev. LaVonne: When you truly believe it is possible, then it is. After all, Spirit put the belief quotient in your mind in the first place, so therefore, it is possible.

Dr. Don: The Apostle Paul wrote: "If we live in the Spirit, let us also walk in the Spirit." (Galatians 5:25)

Rev. LaVonne: To me, knowing this gives comfort. It allows me to relax and remember the truth of the indwelling God.

Dr. Don: Yes. And this awareness can inspire and uplift. What a magnificent creation you are. What a beautiful world God has created for you to enjoy.

Rev. LaVonne: The center of your universe is the center of your Being. How precious it is to know that this innermost point is the blessing of Spirit. Your consciousness and mine overlap. In the mind of God, we are all one.

Both: AND SO IT IS!

Divine Dialogue #31
Spiritually Speaking

Dr. Don: How would your life be different if you constantly spoke with a spiritual consciousness? Rather than phrasing thoughts from a negative viewpoint or strictly from an outer world orientation, what if your words were always positive and stated as if you were actually speaking the thoughts of Spirit?

Rev. LaVonne: At first, this might be challenging. We are constantly hearing negative comments via the media about how you need to go on a diet, have whiter teeth, wear designer clothes and more. Even without hearing the words, body English can telegraph meaning. Not long ago I was in a store that had a TV turned to a teenage type of show. The sound was off, but the 'tween was using facial and bodily expressions that indicated her immense displeasure with the other girl. Each one reflected and reacted to the other in a negative manner.

Dr. Don: Psalm 138:1 says, "How good and how pleasant it is for brethren to dwell together in unity." In our relationships with others, how blessed it is when we speak in supportive, affirming verbiage. We aren't here to compete with each other unless it's to play a game. I believe we are here to uplift one another so that each one of us contributes to life in loving and open-hearted ways. I love seeing people excel in being all they are meant to be.

Rev. LaVonne: So how do you do that? As a child we were taught to "stop, look and listen." That was a guide helping us to safely cross the street. When you hear yourself mutter chatterings that pull you down, stop. Pay attention or look at what you're thinking and listen to that inner voice, Spirit, that always knows the truth about you. You are a perfect child of

God, just as you are.

Dr. Don: This is the kind of thing a person says when they're spiritually speaking. Every word you utter sets into motion an energy that either builds up or tears down. This is especially true of the words you tell yourself. Discover the power of claiming, "I am a perfect child of God. Just as I am." "I am expressing the Spirit of God in everything I say to myself or others."

Rev. LaVonne: John Lennon wrote: "I believe in God, but not as one thing, not as an old man in the sky. I believe that what people call God is something in all of us. I believe that what Jesus and Mohammed and Buddha and all the rest said was right. It's just that the translations have gone wrong." And you have the freedom to choose how to speak and interpret the words you hear and the words you speak.

Dr. Don: Quoting Ernest Holmes: "Let us learn to be still and let the Truth speak to us; to be still and know that the inner light shines." (*The Science of Mind* 369.1)

Both: And so it is.

Divine Dialogue #32
Because We Can

Rev. LaVonne: The Bon Jovi song, *Because We Can* begins "I don't wanna be another wave in the ocean, I am a rock not just another grain of sand." These lyrics inspire me to see the globe as a world that works for everyone, in that we each contribute to the attributes of living.

Dr. Don: God provides us with a vision of a world, where there is an abundance of resources and love, peace and empowerment for all. Our worldwide Centers for Spiritual Living has adopted this vision.

Rev. LaVonne: The idea that we can all work together, respect and appreciate the diversity of one and all, greatly appeals to my sense of being, since at my core I know it is possible. Why? Because we can. And how do we do that?

Dr. Don: When you realize who you are, a Creative Being made in the image and likeness of the Divine, then you can understand that everything you need to fulfill the vision is provided for you. Tell yourself, "I am a Spiritual Being, and all that I need to enjoy a life that works for me and everyone, has already been given, awaiting my acceptance and usage of it."

Rev. LaVonne: Thomas Merton wrote, "A life is either all spiritual or not spiritual at all. No man can serve two masters. Your life is shaped by the end you live for. You are made in the image of what you desire."

Dr. Don: At times, what gets in the way of living your life at the highest level, is getting distracted by problems, outer world issues, or limited beliefs. When you take your focus off the vision of your highest goals, you can get discouraged or upset. Refocusing on the grander picture of what could be, provides the way to getting back on track.

Rev. LaVonne: And in truth, being disturbed or upset may be the very catalyst that you need to change the situation. You can allow yourself to step out of the way and allow Spirit to lead the way. When you trust this process, it is amazing how your life takes on a newer, easier and more joyous hue.

Dr. Don: When you announce a vision or goal to yourself and set your intention on its manifestation in the outer world, the existing structure may get stirred up like mud on the bottom of a pond.

Rev. LaVonne: You allow space for the muck and mire to drain and refill yourself with the cup of kindness mixed with the power of God.

Dr. Don: So, when you claim a world that works for everyone, keeping your eyes on the bigger picture, the vision moves you forward. As the apostle Paul wrote, "I press toward the goal to receive the prize of victory of God's highest calling." (Philippians 3:14)

Rev. LaVonne: Because we can.

Both: And so it is.

Divine Dialogue #33
The Language of Spirit

Rev. LaVonne: "Spirit is always talking to us. We just need to learn the language. I've been learning this language through a translator called Desire." Gina DeGirolamo from our Center wrote those words which inspired this column.

Dr. Don: When you realize that Spirit is love, and love is givingness, your desires tell God what you would like to receive.

Rev. LaVonne: Psalm 37:4 says "Delight yourself in the Lord and He will give you the desires of your heart."

Dr. Don: When you "delight yourself" about someone, you are having a joyous, gracious experience, finding pure delight in their God qualities. When you "delight yourself" in God, you are appreciating the attributes of this Love Energy of the Universe. Focusing on this goodness, you tend to receive even more goodness.

Rev. LaVonne: The desires of the heart are built in. When you have a deep desire to do or accomplish something, that is God speaking to you. Yes, sometimes the language may seem foreign or challenging to understand, yet deep inside I know that Spirit is speaking to each one of us individually, giving us the opportunity to expand ourselves in ways beyond our imagination. That's how Spirit speaks.

Dr. Don: You may be asking, "What if what I am desiring is not really the highest and best for me?" Below the conscious mind, we may not realize that what we think we want may not necessarily be the best for us. In that case, the Universal Presence is still watching your back and may be creating ways to defer the granting of your desire. That's why I sometimes add at end of an affirmative prayer, "This or something better is now manifesting for my highest good."

Rev. LaVonne: Since God dwells and has its being in the center of everyone, your heart's desire is just the beginning of a way to live with purpose and fulfillment. When you allow your creative thoughts and ideas to flourish, you are acting as a conduit for Spirit to do its work. To quote Ayn Rand, "A creative man is motivated by the desire to achieve, not by the desire to beat others."

Dr. Don: When you are listening for Divine guidance, ask, "What wants to happen here and what is it I desire for a greater life?" Then sit quietly, and listen for an answer. It may be an insight, an inspiration, a deep yearning or something else. Let the answer present itself.

Rev. LaVonne: When you remember that God is always there for you, life's little lumps smooth out and the path to happiness seems less bumpy.

Dr. Don: An interesting thing happens when you identify a desire. You get a hint of something God wants to give you. By focusing on the gift, there is a Force that is set into motion to co-create it. As Ernest Holmes wrote, "We have to provide within ourselves a mental and spiritual likeness for the thing desired. Whatever is imagined is brought forth from mind into manifestation."

Both: And so it is.

Divine Dialogue #34
Just Ask

Rev. LaVonne: When I was a child in Sunday School, our teacher had us play a game. We would think of a question, then open the Bible and point to a passage. The teacher helped us figure out what was written.

Dr. Don: I just now tried it and turned to Matthew 21:22 which says, "And everything that you will ask in prayer believing, you shall receive." Pretty amazing, since our topic is, "Just Ask."

Rev. LaVonne: And that's how it works. In truth, since you are one with Spirit, every question you have in your mind has already been formulated by Spirit. So, when you have either a small or a large question to have answered, just ask Spirit.

Dr. Don: Is there something you would like to have in your life? Just ask Spirit. The Love Energy of the Universe wants good for you, and your part is to ask and accept, believing in the intention and power of God to provide. Does that mean you can have somebody else's house or car or spouse? No. Spirit provides that which you desire so long as it harms no one and is good for all.

Rev. LaVonne: Ernest Holmes wrote, "As we express life, we fulfill God's law of abundance, but we do this only as we realize that there is good enough to go around - only as we know that all of God's gifts are given as freely and fully as the air and the sunshine...alike to all."

Dr. Don: So, if you have not been experiencing the gifts freely and fully, why not? Have you asked? How have you asked? If you say, "You wouldn't want to help me, would you?" you are affirming the negative. The way to ask effectively, is to know God always wants to give, that you deserve the best, then gratefully accept that which you deserve and desire.

Rev. LaVonne: Does this work? You bet. Recently, I noticed a comment on the bottom of the receipt of the coffee shop where we write our column. It stated that you could earn rewards for your purchases. When I asked the clerk about it she gave us a "Loyalty Royalty Club" card and stamped all ten boxes saying, "You two come in all the time; you're next drink is free."

Dr. Don: The complimentary mocha smoothie I ordered the next time tasted better than usual, which brings up another element of receiving blessings: appreciation. You receive more for that for which you are grateful. I give thanks for perfect health, my loving relationship, joyful experiences with family and spiritual friends, prosperity, wisdom, happiness, comfortable living, and the pleasant climate and beauty of the Central Coast.

Rev. LaVonne: Just for today, test it out for yourself. Set your intention, consult Spirit and watch what happens when you just ask.

Both: And so it is.

Divine Dialogue #35
Spiritual Wellness

Dr. Don: While modern medicine may reflect the wisdom of the Universal Spirit in providing humanity with enhanced health and new techniques of detection, diagnosis, treatment and maintenance of wellness, the ultimate healer is God.

Rev. LaVonne: You don't need to try to stay well, because in reality God has already made you perfect. Cardinal Newman noted, "Here below to be human is to change. And to be perfect is to have changed often."

Dr. Don: "The spiritual man [person] needs no healing...God is in and through every man [one] and...this Indwelling Presence is already perfect," according to Ernest Holmes.

Rev. LaVonne: So, if this is true why do people get sick?

Dr. Don: God gives you leeway to choose. In the cosmic soup of divine wholeness lies the potential for its opposite. You make the choice, and you might make it unconsciously. For example, you may have witnessed a sick parent and identified with the ailment so much that you attracted the disease.

Rev. LaVonne: The proof of Spirit is in the healing. Every child has fallen down, skinned a knee or cut their finger. Within seconds the body begins to heal, within days the skin is back together and soon the fall is forgotten. The Spirit body knows how to heal itself.

Dr. Don: You have heard, "Anything you pray for and ask, believe that you will receive it, and it will be done for you." (Mark 11:24) The Life Force provides a tendency for healing to happen and provides the wisdom and guidance to know how to enhance the healing, whether it be through changing your diet, exercising, consulting a doctor or an alternative therapist, or by modifying your belief.

Rev. LaVonne: Everyone has a belief in something, even those who claim not to believe in a Spiritual entity have a belief in that. Since we're talking about wellness, it is my belief that an escalated life-style, one filled with stress, leans toward an unbalanced mind and body. When that happens, the body reacts in the form of illness.

Dr. Don: Once the body gives you a symptom which is the feedback that something is out of balance, you can then counter it by remembering that Spirit does the healing. You deserve to be well and your belief creates you as whole, complete and perfect.

Rev. LaVonne: Stress in and of itself is not the problem; a certain amount of stress is a motivating source for getting things accomplished. It's our reaction to stressful situations that clog up our minds and bodies. Effective tools like meditation, being still, feeling oneness with nature and praying, can bring you back to your Source: God.

Dr. Don: Affirmations, repeated often, also penetrate deep into your mind to provide repetitive messages about your true self. Repeat something like "God's the wholeness that I am."

Rev. LaVonne: Relax, enjoy the process and feel the Spirit within you rejoice.

Both: And so it is.

Divine Dialogue #36
The Heart of Stress

Dr. Don: Many doctors say, the top two fatal health challenges are cancer and heart related issues. Research shows that behind both these and many other health challenges is stress.

Rev. LaVonne: According to two doctors who wrote the book *None of These Diseases,* "At the dawn of the third millennium, health enemy number one is stress both, spiritual and mental."

Dr. Don: S.I. Mc Millen, M.D. and David E. Stern, M.D. claim, "people are more than chemicals and chemical reactions; people are spiritual beings."

Rev. LaVonne: Knowing, trusting and totally believing the innate spiritual truth within, I know Spirit is at the heart of your being and knows how to heal and make you whole.

Dr. Don: Trace it back: Behind many health issues is stress, behind stress is feeling out of control of conditions.

Rev. LaVonne: The Director of the Institute of Stress, Dr. Robert Eliot says, "Tell me how much control a person has over what he really wants and I'll tell you how much stress he has."

Dr. Don: Behind control is a feeling of separation from the Presence of the Mind of God. Ernest Holmes said, "I believe in the healing of the sick...and the control of conditions through the Power of this Mind."

Rev. LaVonne: Mind is God. God created all of us, including our minds. The solution to the challenge of letting go of having to control is to turn yourself over to God.

Dr. Don: Quoting Psalm 120:1, "In my distress I cried to the Lord, and he heard me." When you feel connected to that Creative Spirit, it restores peace of mind and a healthy body. That's the heart of it all.

Rev. LaVonne: When I was in high school we had to write a report about health. There were no books in the school library concerning stress. Finally, I found an article in *Time Magazine* written about Hans Selye.

Dr. Don: His work has led to volumes of research, writings and practical applications of his findings.

Rev. LaVonne: Dr. Selye noted that stress is stress whether it's good or bad. He coined the word stress calling negative stress "distress" and positive stress "eustress."

Dr. Don: You need a certain level of stress researchers call "optimum stress" in order to maintain a healthy interest in life.

Rev. LaVonne: In order to direct your energy positively, trust Spirit. Let God, at the heart of your being, lead the way and de-stress yourself.

Dr. Don: Syndicated television talk show hostess, Queen Latifah, uses her own stress-reduction ritual before going in front of the cameras.

Rev. LaVonne: She comments, "I say a prayer, meet the guests and go rock the show." Why not rock your show? Start with prayer, listen to your God-voice and let go. Watch what happens. You may be amazed.

Both: And so it is.

Divine Dialogue #37
When Elephants Fly

Rev. LaVonne: Did you ever have an idea then thought to yourself, "Impossible. What makes me think I can do that?"

Dr. Don: Amazing and sometimes seemingly miraculous achievements have been created through the use of possibility thinking. Walt Disney was a great example of someone who used this kind of thinking. He said, "It's kind of fun to do the impossible."

Rev. LaVonne: The truth is, the idea originates in the mind, and the mind is part of God's creation. Each of us is different and unique with endless possibilities of creativity. Your ability to discover, invent and tap into your inner resources is always available. Again quoting Mr. Disney, "If you can dream it, you can do it."

Dr. Don: You are also given a mind that can discern the viability of a given project. You learn from life experiences and Divine Wisdom supports you in evaluating the likelihood of fulfillment. It's important to keep an open mind. Ernest Holmes writes, "Never limit your view of life by any past experience. The possibility of life is inherent within the capacity to imagine what life is, backed by the power to produce this imagery, or Divine Imagination. It is not a question of failing or succeeding. It is simply a question of sticking to an idea until it becomes a tangible reality."

Rev. LaVonne: As a child I had a dream of becoming a professional actress on the stage, television and in movies. The belief that I could do that was always in my mind. For years I performed for free, giving me an opportunity to learn from the ground up. Then, after my children left the nest, I did too. Currently, I'm acting in films, TV and commercials and fulfilling those dreams in Los Angeles. Dreams can only fade with your permission.

Dr. Don: When I was a boy, my favorite Disney character was Dumbo, (since my left ear stuck out.) A small mouse named Timothy convinced Dumbo that with his big ears, he could fly. I believe there is a "still, small voice" within each of us that whispers what is possible. By ignoring the opinions of others, and listening to that inner voice, you can let the highest ideas become a reality. Just remember to keep your eye on the goal. Keep that vision of what is possible foremost in your mind. Your greatest potentialities can become realities.

Rev. LaVonne: Maybe you've heard that some things are so fantastical that they can't happen. The saying is something like, "Oh yeah? When pigs fly!" An elephant is a lot heavier than a pig and Dumbo believed he could fly, so he did. Why not let your thoughts fly and soar to the sky? You're never alone, God is always ready to support your course.

Dr. Don: "With God, all things are possible." (Matthew 19:26) Even my left ear is now perfect!

Both: And so it is.

Divine Dialogue #38
What Am I Thinking?

Rev. LaVonne: There's a saying that people use today: "What were you thinking?" Several years ago a board game of the same name won a "Best Abstract Game Award." The creator, Richard Garfield, wrote as the subtitle to the game: "It's not whether you win or lose, it's how you think the same."

Dr. Don: Human beings think. We have the ability to use logic and make choices. Yet, we are all different.

Rev. LaVonne: General Patton said: "If everyone is thinking alike, then somebody isn't thinking." The beauty is that we are all connected by the same Universal Mind, the Mind of God. And yes, we have individualized thoughts that derive from the same Mind.

Dr. Don: I find it interesting that you can be aware of your thoughts. You can hear what you're saying. I notice that negative or positive experiences in my life show up in accordance with my thoughts.

Rev. LaVonne: The Creator made us in the image and likeness of the Divine. So you use the same power to create as Spirit. The whole universe came into being through God.

Dr. Don: And in your life, you have the ability to create the circumstances you want to experience. To the degree that you choose similar circumstances as Spirit, life for you is good.

Rev. LaVonne: Sometimes people inadvertently create experiences they really did not want. The same creative process takes instruction from negative thoughts, ideas and beliefs and duplicates them in the outer world.

Dr. Don: In *How to Use the Science of Mind,* Ernest Holmes wrote, "We are using a principle which automatically reacts to us by corresponding with our mental attitudes. Jesus affirmed this when he said, 'It is done unto you as you believe'."

Rev. LaVonne: When an incident happens that is surprisingly contrary to the beautiful life you thought you were choosing to live, you might ask yourself, "What was I thinking?"

Dr. Don: In a sense, thoughts are things. It's not that you need to worry about every fleeting negative thought. Holmes claims it is the majority of your thinking that tends to manifest in the outer world. That's 51% of your total beliefs, thoughts and attitudes.

Rev. LaVonne: In the book, *The Untethered Soul,* Michael A. Singer identifies the nature of a person as that which is conscious of all the conditions, emotions and thoughts that you have. He says, "You are behind everything, just watching. That is your true home."

Dr. Don: As you become conscious of the content of your thoughts, you are in a position to change them and thereby change the resultant events and circumstances.

Rev. LaVonne: As you notice what's on your mind, you can predict what's being created and make positive choices. "Old things have passed away." (II Corinthians 5:17)

Dr. Don: Through your Divine nature, all things become new. Let the blessings of life be on your mind and you are automatically blessed.

Both: And so it is.

Divine Dialogue #39
Whatever You Choose

Dr. Don: The ability to choose, is a central theme in the New Thought teaching. You can choose how you refer to God: Creator, Spirit, the Divine, Love, the One, Universal Mind and more.

Rev. LaVonne: As a Native American Indian, I choose those roots and call my Inner Guide, The Great Spirit. The Truth is, God, by any other name, is still the life-force, the energy, the reason for you living as a Spiritual Being.

Dr. Don: You have a choice about how you refer to your own Spiritual nature in relation to God. You can think of it as Christ, the Buddha nature, the Atman (in Hinduism), the Holy Spirit, the I Am nature, the Divine within or any other label that makes you feel one with God.

Rev. LaVonne: The reason most people seek out a Spiritual Path is to ease the disharmonies of life. Groucho Marx said: "I, not events, have the power to make me happy or unhappy today. I choose which it shall be. Yesterday is dead, tomorrow hasn't arrived yet. I have just one day, today and I'm going to be happy in it."

Dr. Don: I think the most important choice you can make is whether or not you choose to be happy. If you have truly made that choice, you won't let anything get in the way of happiness, even the worst problems or circumstances. Choosing happiness is a powerful way to lead your life and there is an easy way to get started. Pray.

Rev. LaVonne: When you pray, you are choosing qualities, circumstances and infinite possibilities. God always provides.

Dr. Don: God has an abundance of love, wholeness, wisdom, and even material things for your enjoyment. By praying affirmatively and being specific about your preferences (without outlining, that is, telling God how to do it), your Spiritual life expands.

Rev. LaVonne: It's also important to release any attachment to the outcome and allow Spirit to do It's work.

Dr. Don: Ernest Holmes makes it clear that you can pray for whatever you choose, "so long as it harms no one." Of course, your Spiritual nature wouldn't want to harm anyone. Your nature is God's nature. You are Love.

Rev. LaVonne: When you remember to approach life with love in mind, the path of happiness becomes natural. In the process, smile and watch your joy spread to others.

Dr. Don: Isaiah 7:15 says, "Choose the good." Yet, how do you know for sure what's good for yourself and others? I like to add to my affirmative prayers, "This or something better now manifests in the outer world as I accept the highest and best."

Rev. LaVonne: When you have a moment of darkness, when your world seems to be falling apart, turn on your Inner Light. The Light of God. It is always available, just switch your thoughts and turn on your God-switch.

Both: And so it is.

Divine Dialogue #40
In Tune with the Infinite

Rev. LaVonne: "There is a golden thread that runs through every religion of the world." Those are the words of philosopher and author Ralph Waldo Trine. This idea warms my heart, since I believe we are all connected through The Infinite.

Dr. Don: I like referring to God as The Infinite. It gives me a feeling of awe in realizing that all of the qualities of the Divine Spirit are unlimited. The One is the Source of infinite love, power, wisdom, wholeness, and creative energy. Most importantly, the Infinite must be everywhere without limit and therefore It must be inclusive of all that I am. God incarnates in and through you and me.

Rev. LaVonne: The infinity symbol, that of a sideways numeral 8, basically describes something without any limit. This resonates to me to be like God. Limitless, always available, boundless. Within you are infinite God qualities.

Dr. Don: In Psalm 147:5, it says "Great is our Lord, and great is his power; his understanding is infinite." All of the God qualities are infinite and we share them all. You can tune into that same power, love, wisdom, joy and wholeness. It's a matter of degree. How much of the infinite good can you accept?

Rev. LaVonne: When you have an idea, an inspired thought, guess where that comes from? God. Think of all the thoughts you've had through the years. Have you acted on them? Even if its just one little move toward your goal, the time to move forward is in the moment. This moment is part of the eternal now.

Dr. Don: You can experience the eternal now by being in tune with the Infinite. When you are in tune, you are living in the atmosphere and consciousness of that Divine Energy. So every spiritual tool moves you to a higher and more complete awareness of the Presence. And when you are more aware, you attract greater good because you are that good.

Rev. LaVonne: Louise L. Hay writes, "Remember, in the vast infinity of life, all is perfect, whole and complete...and so are you." The challenge is remembering to remember who you truly are. An easy way is to just stop, be still in your mind, release all thoughts and let God take over. Yes, God knows what to do next.

Dr. Don: Are you like the fish, looking for the water when all the time it's swimming through it and the water is moving through the fish? Spirit is moving through you and you are immersed in Spirit. Just go with the flow. Your consciousness is God consciousness.

Rev. LaVonne: "Flow with whatever is happening and let your mind be free. Stay centered by accepting whatever you are doing. This is the ultimate." (Chang Tzu)

Both: And so it is.

Divine Dialogue #41
The God Particle

Dr. Don: Have you heard that the Nobel Prize in Physics has been awarded to the scientists who discovered what has been nicknamed the "The God Particle?"

Rev. LaVonne: Such exciting news. I've always known there is a God and to know it, is dazzling.

Dr. Don: The subatomic particle called Higgs boson is what gives mass to matter. This is an over-simplified definition of a long studied phenomenon that deserves deeper understanding.

Rev. LaVonne: Everything is energy. I believe this energy is directly derived from Spirit. The interconnectedness of all planets, places and things is powerful and meant to be. You have the ability to expand your universe by tapping into the Divine at any moment.

Dr. Don: Albert Einstein was interested in the relationship of energy and matter with his famous formula, E=mc squared. The amount of energy is equal to the mass multiplied by the speed of light multiplied by itself. That's a lot of energy. I think that's a commentary on the magnitude of God.

Rev. LaVonne: The magnitude of God can be proven by merely looking around. Look at the countless stars, the many grains of sand, the immensity of space and the possibilities of endless love. It's all good and it's all God. Helen Keller said: "The best and most beautiful things in the world cannot be seen or even touched - they must be felt with the heart."

Dr. Don: It's good that scientists attempt to find the cause of everything through what they know, yet until they know with their hearts that the energy back of everything is Divine energy, they won't really find the cause. Ernest Holmes wrote, "God is the invisible energy Life Essence of all that is, the Intelligent Energy running through all. This Life we *feel* but do not see."

Rev. LaVonne: Not long ago, we attended a Ministers Gathering in Napa, California. While riding our bikes through a parking lot we noticed a parking space with the word "Compassion" painted on it. At first, I thought it was someone's last name. Then we noticed seven other labeled parking spaces.

Dr. Don: They were: Community, Honor, Commitment, Integrity, Respect, Charity and Gratitude.

Rev. LaVonne: We went into the restaurant and asked the manager about the words and found out an art show had used the lot and were granted permission to enhance the spaces.

Dr. Don: These words uplift those who park in the spaces, creating a positive energy. So also, the word of God constantly creates. "Everything came to be by his hand; and without him not even one thing that was created came to be." (John 1:3) And this creation continues to be.

Rev. LaVonne: The words you use are powerful, which is why it's important to enhance your life positively. The invisible energy manifests as you give it direction.

Dr. Don: There is a part of you that is the God Particle.

Both: And so it is.

Divine Dialogue #42
Faith without Fear

Rev. LaVonne: "Love is what we were born with. Fear is what we learned here." Those words are expressed by author and spiritual teacher, Marianne Williamson. Some have learned the fear game real well. To me, the opposite of fear is love. And God is perfect love.

Dr. Don: The same energy as fear can be transmuted into faith. Scripture affirms "Perfect love casts out fear." (1John 4:18) God's love provides a way to deal with any negative emotion. In the presence of love, anything unlike itself is dissipated and all that remains is God.

Rev. LaVonne: I recall a *Bizarro* cartoon that showed a group of smiling children waiting to break a piñata. The balloon over the piñata said: "Do not concern yourself with what is inside me; it is what's inside YOU that truly matters." And that's the truth. The presence of God dwells within everything and everyone equally.

Dr. Don: That's the reason you can use faith as a tool for improving your experience of life. As you have faith in God's intention for you to be healthy, wealthy, happy and wise, you attract those experiences. Then, as you see the positive results of faith, it increases your ability to accept better and better experiences.

Rev. LaVonne: So what's to fear? There is a built-in power of survival that allows you to continue the work of God on Mother Earth. You embody Spirit and have the ability to overcome any fear. A newspaper article reported of a 72 year old man who survived 19 days in the Mendocino National Forest. He said, "I didn't panic because panic will kill me right away. I knew that."

Dr. Don: I think he also knew he would survive. You can do more than just survive when you use faith. When you remember that God is love and Spirit provides all the blessings of a joyful and uplifting life, your faith makes it so.

Rev. LaVonne: Ernest Holmes said, "Faith has been recognized as a power throughout the ages - whether it be faith in God, faith in one's fellowman, in oneself, or in what one is doing. Those who have great faith, have great power."

Dr. Don: Those who have a faith, using the word as a noun, are happier. Several studies prove the correlation between spirituality and happiness. Highly spiritual people, are twice as likely to say they are "very happy."

Rev. LaVonne: It's all a choice. When you choose to eliminate fear and choose to be happy, your life changes. A local bank handed out postcards that read: "A smile is the leading cause of happiness."

Dr. Don: My belief in a Higher Power is one that gives unconditionally. I choose to accept.

Rev. LaVonne: Recognizing the gifts of God, accepting the Divine abundance, then being proactively productive is a non-fear formula for happiness.

Both: And so it is.

Divine Dialogue #43
Back in Time

Dr. Don: At least twice a year you get to see how fleeting time is - how you can just change the clock and make it a different time. Time is relative. You can make a lot of choices about your relationship to time.

Rev. LaVonne: In truth, you can change the clock to whatever time you want, yet in this part of the country, day would still be day and night would still be night.

Dr. Don: Genesis 1:5 says, "And God called the light day, and the darkness he called night." The system we use is based upon the rotation of the earth and the relative position of where we live compared to the position of the Sun.

Rev. LaVonne: "In the natural process of evolution, what we call time elapses - one day, one week, one month, one year - but in Spirit, there is no time. The Spirit is timeless." (Ernest Holmes)

Dr. Don: Yet, Spirit is apparently aware of time, otherwise how can you account for synchronous events? How do coincidences come to be? How can your spiritual nature participate in these activities and in what way do you play a part in their creation?

Rev. LaVonne: "Living in the moment" and "living in the now" are common phrases today. Yes, it is a way to live a less convoluted life, yet it's important to reflect on the past and make plans for the future.

Dr. Don: You make decisions all the time about time. You say, "I'm a night person" or "I'm a morning person." Others may observe you as always being on time or always late. You're in a position of power because you're the chooser.

Rev. LaVonne: A few years ago, one of my grandchildren wanted to interview me for a school project. He asked: "Momo, what was it like in the olden days?" Olden days? What? Me? Then I realized that life from his viewpoint had progressed rapidly and my past was something of interest.

Dr. Don: Did you ever wish you could go back in time to change a choice? If you could see from the point of view of the future you might want to change it.

Rev. LaVonne: Kahlil Gibran wrote: "Time has been transformed, and we have changed; it has advanced and set us in motion; it has unveiled its face, inspiring us with bewilderment and exhilaration."

Dr. Don: What if you were to approach everything from the point of Spirit? Maybe you have an upcoming meeting and you remember to pray first for the good of all parties.

Rev. LaVonne: By putting God in the center of your life, in every situation and event, you can change your experiences of the past, present and future.

Dr. Don: Use your power of imagination to shift the energy. You are more powerful than you know.

Rev. LaVonne: Oh yes, remember to set your clocks back (or forward) when the time comes.

Both: And so it is.

Divine Dialogue #44
Illumination

Rev. LaVonne: Have you ever noticed how when some people enter a room, it seems to literally light up?

Dr. Don: Many illumined beings have demonstrated that a spiritually uplifted consciousness appears as a light.

Rev. LaVonne: Spiritual or intellectual enlightenment leads to deeper insight and understanding about this life experience on planet earth and beyond.

Dr. Don: Ernest Holmes commented, "Illumination will come as man more and more realizes his Unity with the Whole, and as he constantly endeavors to let the Truth operate through him."

Rev. LaVonne: The Whole means God, as does the word Truth. I believe that since Spirit is everywhere and within everyone, at your core you are whole, perfect and complete.

Dr. Don: When you align with that wholeness, you are one with the Light of Spirit. More than a hundred years ago, Maurice Bucke wrote *Cosmic Consciousness* in which he identified dozens of people who he felt had been so illumined that they expressed this heightened level of spiritual vibration. Of course, the great spiritual masters were on his list, including Lao Tzu, Buddha, Jesus and many others.

Rev. LaVonne: When you recognize the greatness of others you are allowing your own greatness to shine. In a way, it's like you are a moon that reflects the light of the sun. "We can easily forgive a child who is afraid of the dark; the real tragedy of life is when men are afraid of the light." (Plato)

Dr. Don: In Matthew, you'll find the story of the illumination of Jesus. Two of his disciples witnessed it and reported, "...and his face shone like the sun, and his clothes turned white like light." (Matthew 17:2) Since Jesus indicated that you can do those things he did, illumination is within the possibilities for you to achieve. Apparently, you are to lift your consciousness to a higher level as symbolized by the high mountain to which Jesus ascended.

Rev. LaVonne: How do you do that? Here are several suggestions.
· Get out of your own way and pray; let God guide you.
· Release attachment to the outcome; listen to Spirit by learning to meditate.
· Allow your inner thoughts to fly, by journaling.

Dr. Don: The use of these spiritual tools makes room for you to let your light gleam. Allow it to happen; you are already "the light of the world." Relax and glow in your Divine nature. Just be.

Rev. LaVonne: Rest in the comfort of the arms of Spirit. You are never, ever alone. Spirit is always with you. Your presence is the presence of God. Be the illuminance of Spirit.

Dr. Don: When you know these truths and let your life be guided by them, you are enlightened. This state of being can be easy. You have been given everything you need to live fully in joy, love, peace and enlightenment. Enjoy.

Both: And so it is.

Divine Dialogue #45
Honoring Those Who Serve

Rev. LaVonne: On Veterans' Day, we honor those men and women who have served our blessed country in the military.

Dr. Don: Whenever you choose to serve others, you are using a divine quality and duplicating the nature of God. To serve is to love and it is love that you express when you give of yourself. I am touched at a deep level when someone gives unselfishly, thereby blessing my life.

Rev. LaVonne: Many years ago while living on the Monterey Peninsula I directed a play at the Naval Postgraduate School. One of the actors was a Lieutenant Commander who was shot down in North Vietnam. He was just thirty years old. He was held captive for two years. There were bracelets engraved with the name of the Prisoner of War. I still have the one I wore in honor of this man. When he was released he commented: "Continue to seek out the truth, and keep the spirit of unity, which makes this country great, moving and growing. God bless you all."

Dr. Don: The spirit of unity is the reason something stirs within when someone serves at this level. It is that spirit that is Divine, connecting everyone, and calling forth a greater level of givingness.

Rev. LaVonne: John Doolittle said, "America's Veterans have served their country with the belief that democracy and freedom are ideals to be upheld around the world."

Dr. Don: Whoever supports a military person is honorable as well, including the mates and families of Veterans. Whole nations are called to give of themselves. I think respect and admiration of those who serve can expand to include teachers, ministers, social workers, government employees, financial supporters and many other givers. I choose to say "thank you" to all of them.

Rev. LaVonne: It's natural to want to give. In fact, I believe the law of giving and receiving is a dynamic exchange of energy. Giving and receiving co-exist. The source, of course, is God. Nature is an example of divine giving. Plants grow, we eat some of them and the plant continues to give. We receive the gift and in turn we are caretakers of the land and of the animals of Mother Earth.

Dr. Don: When you function in balance and in a centered relationship with Mother Earth, your life in infinitely blessed. "He which soweth sparingly shall reap also sparingly; and he which soweth bountifully shall reap also bountifully." (II Corinthians 9:6)

Rev. LaVonne: The bottom line is love. God is love; love is God. Ernest Holmes wrote: "Love is self-givingness through creation, the impartation of the Divine through the human." That is where we Spiritual Beings fit in.

Dr. Don: I know that the love of Spirit surrounds every Veteran right now. I am aligned and supportive of their willingness to give. May we all celebrate and love their inner truth and light.

Both: And so it is.

Divine Dialogue #46
Grateful for a Thankful Spirit

Rev. LaVonne: Thanksgiving Day is coming soon. Not everyone looks forward to it because not everyone has wonderful Thanksgiving Holiday experiences. As a Native American I have different feelings about how we honor our heritage.

Dr. Don: I think it's good that we set aside a day to give thanks and get together with family and/or friends to enjoy a delicious Thanksgiving meal. Those of us who have this kind of positive experience, can be grateful. I am even more thankful for the ability to create joyful experiences all the time, because out of a consciousness of thankfulness, life responds and provides unlimited blessings every day.

Rev. LaVonne: Here's a little history. Originally, the newly arrived English colonists were greeted by a Wampanoag Indian named Squanto. He spoke English and became an interpreter; the English Separatists were taught how to hunt, fish, gather and cultivate food for survival. Eventually, a celebration of gratitude was shared by both factions.

Dr. Don: All major religions of the world teach the importance of gratitude.

Rev. LaVonne: Spending quality time with others and in nature is a way to experience thankfulness. From the time I was a child, I learned from my father to always express gratitude to Mother Earth.

Dr. Don: There's a similar idea expressed in First Thessalonians 5:17-18, "Pray without ceasing; In all things give thanks..."

Rev. LaVonne: Here is a Thanksgiving address given by the Haudenosaunee also known as The Five Nations of the Iroquois. "With one mind, we turn to honor and thank all the food plants we harvest from the garden. Since the beginning of time, the grains, vegetables, beans and berries have helped the people survive. Many other living things draw strength from them too. We gather all the plant foods together as one and send them a greeting of thanks."

Dr. Don: Rather than waiting until the big feast prayer, how about making it a habit to live in a spirit of gratitude every day, every hour, every minute. By doing so, you'll find yourself opening to joys of every kind.

Rev. LaVonne: Another way is to give to someone else. One year my children and I went to the Fairgrounds in Monterey, California that served food to the homeless. It is a memory we'll always remember with humility, gratitude and love. I like what W. J. Cameron wrote: "Thanksgiving, after all is a word of action."

Dr. Don: No matter what method you use to express gratitude, there is always a return. After all, the Universe never grows weary of giving to you and never runs out of the good you may receive. Ernest Holmes wrote, "It is as though we were dipping up water from a limitless sea. Each day we may use a larger measure and each day dip up more. The ocean will never become exhausted."

Rev. LaVonne: I'm grateful to be thankful and to know that the Spirit within you and me constantly expresses.

Both: And so it is.

Divine Dialogue #47
The Gift of Healing

Dr. Don: As you enter into the Holiday season, do you anticipate colorful decorations, shopping, family fun and good times? There may also be overcrowded stores, busy schedules, and physical or mental stress.

Rev. LaVonne: How you approach this Season of Light and Love is important in maintaining perfect health. The Spirit that dwells within already knows how to be whole; it's up to you to remember to tap into that inner Divinity.

Dr. Don: "Do not imitate the way of the world, but be transformed by the renewal of your minds, that you may discern what is that good and acceptable and perfect will of God." (Romans 12:2) It's God's intention for you to be healthy.

Rev. LaVonne: How do you start? Just breathe. Relax, release and let go. Become detached from the outcome and allow God to be your guide. Another way is to laugh. See the humor in situations.

Dr. Don: Healing chemicals are released in the brain when you laugh. Laughter also relieves residual stress. Sickness does not have a power of its own. As you choose wellness, your immune system responds to the healing power of Spirit.

Rev. LaVonne: Do you have to be sick, injured or incomplete to be healed? The word healing really means whole, and since your Spirit is never sick, you can experience a new freedom of being complete. "Healing does not mean going back to the way things were before, but rather allowing what is now to move us closer to God." (Ram Dass)

Dr. Don: There is power in focusing on the *now* moment. As you live *now*, you are in the divine present. By letting go of past problems and ceasing to worry about the future, immeasurable energy is freed to live wholly (holy).

Rev. LaVonne: Beyond physical wholeness is the purity of Spiritual wholeness. It is an inborn gift of Spirit.

Dr. Don: At the core of your being is perfection, the spirit of God. When you remove any barriers to expressing that wholeness, such as a belief in sickness or other false ideas, your natural health is uncovered and revealed.

Rev. LaVonne: What a relief to know that all I have to do is to be in alignment with my true self, my God-self.

Dr. Don: If there are moments of doubt or false beliefs as you move through the busy holidays, use spiritual tools such as affirmative prayer, meditation and affirmations to restore your consciousness to the truth of wholeness.

Rev. LaVonne: Practicing these techniques is God's gift that we can also pass along to others.

Dr. Don: "There is that within every individual which partakes of the nature of the Universal Wholeness and - in so far as it operates - is God. That is the meaning of the word *Emmanuel,* the meaning of the word *Christ.*" (Ernest Holmes)

Rev. LaVonne: Let's celebrate the holy gifts of healing.

Both: And so it is.

Divine Dialogue #48
The Gift of Abundance

Dr. Don: What if you had all of the abundance that would contribute to making your Holiday Season more joyful than you ever imagined? What if you could shop without limitations and share your prosperity unhampered by budgetary concerns?

Rev. LaVonne: Stephen R. Covey wrote, "An abundance mentality springs from internal security, not from external rankings, comparisons, opinions, possessions, or associations." What this tells me, is that with God at my core, I am filled with abundant possibilities.

Dr. Don: The truth is that you are already prosperous. God has already provided an ample supply of everything that makes life worthwhile, letting you choose the level of abundance that your desire. It's up to you to accept it. It's also up to you to let Divine Intelligence guide you in the methods in which your prosperity manifests in your life.

Rev. LaVonne: An article in the *Science of Mind* magazine told of a minister, Rev. Joe Hooper who traveled to Bali. Even though many of the people were living in poverty, he was impressed with how at peace they were. Their focus was not on lack but on all that God provides. They also are committed to sharing what they have by giving offerings of flowers and incense several times a day. They live in faith.

Dr. Don: Yes, certainly the season isn't about money, or how expensive the gifts are that you give. As in every area of life, what's important is putting God first. Love must be the spirit behind the giving. The gift given with unconditional generosity is the best gift of all.

Rev. LaVonne: "Love and compassion are necessities, not luxuries. Without them, humanity cannot survive." (The Dalai Lama)

Dr. Don: There is a direct relationship between the two. As you give, the level of abundance that is given to you increases without limitation. "My cup runneth over." (Psalm 23:5) If you find yourself experiencing lack, look for areas where there may be a belief in scarcity or reservations about giving. Decide to change your beliefs and you will change your experience.

Rev. LaVonne: Maybe you can start by doing something small. You could take a moment, and write a list of all the things for which you are grateful. If that seems daunting, then just name three.

Dr. Don: What would be special for your favorite aunt; a phone call, a letter, more of your time, a memory? What would enrich her life? I had an aunt that always sent me a handkerchief. I would have preferred a word of praise.

Rev. LaVonne: Yes, those are the gifts of love. Within you, me, our pets and more are undeniable gifts of Spirit. At this time of year, let's be reminded to give of ourselves and celebrate the gift of giving.

Both: And so it is.

Divine Dialogue #49
The Gift of Wisdom

Rev. LaVonne: At first I laughed when I read this quote by John Wolfgang von Goete: "Ignorant men raise questions that wise men answered a thousand years ago," then I realized the wisdom of those words.

Dr. Don: Wisdom is a gift from the Creator which everyone may use to guide all areas of living. You can make the choice to listen, understand and apply that inner wisdom and bless your life.

Rev. LaVonne: The potential for wisdom is already within you and me and everyone we know. Several years ago when one of my granddaughters was four years old, I asked: "What do you want to be when you grow up?" She answered "A-dult." It took me a moment to get what she meant. Being an adult and handling some of life's challenges requires taking on responsibilities.

Dr. Don: What if you could rely on an inner wisdom, a knowingness, a realization of Truth and an understanding of higher wisdom every time you needed to make an important decision?

Rev. LaVonne: The truth is that inner wisdom is always there and is ready for you to turn to it and receive the guidance.

Dr. Don: The prophets of scripture seemed to possess this trait; Solomon was renowned for his remarkable wisdom in guiding the Israelites.

Rev. LaVonne: In fact, the whole book of Proverbs is said to be authored by King Solomon. He wrote, "A wise man will listen and will increase learning; and a man of understanding shall attain to leadership." (Proverb 1:5)

Dr. Don: The Bible refers to man as mankind and we can interpret that to mean men and women. All sentient beings can learn from these teachings.

Rev. LaVonne: Sometimes when I'm faced with a choice of how to react to a situation, I'll think of a person whom I consider to be really wise. It removes me from an emotional equation and allows my wisdom-self to flourish. It's also of value to just get quiet. A Cherokee prayer reads, "O' Great Spirit, help me always to speak the truth quietly, to listen with an open mind when others speak, and to remember the peace that may be found in silence."

Dr. Don: Meditation is an empowering spiritual tool through which discernment, decision-making and Divine guidance can bring great clarity. Even a quick inner glance can reveal the answer from deep within.

Rev. LaVonne: Quoting American philosopher Ernest Holmes, "The Divine Mind is infinite. It contains all knowledge and wisdom, but, before It can reveal Its secrets, It must have an outlet. This outlet we shall be compelled to supply through our own receptive mentalities."

Dr. Don: When you receive communication from that "still, small voice" within, the immense presence of Spirit is available and you can act from a God-centered point.

Rev. LaVonne: To use your inner power is living with Spiritual Wisdom. How very wise.

Both: And so it is.

Divine Dialogue #50
The Gift of Creativity

Dr. Don: Do you think Santa will bring you the gift of creativity for Christmas? Everyone has the ability to create, to be different from others. The possibilities are endless.

Rev. LaVonne: Maya Angelou wrote: "You cannot use up creativity. The more you use, the more you have."

Dr. Don: It's important to express your individualized creativity which contributes to living purposefully and joyfully.

Rev. LaVonne: Have you ever been so deeply involved in a project that you forgot where you were, what time it was and not even noticed that you were hungry? I have, many times, especially when I was sitting at my sewing machine.

Dr. Don: In the past, I have felt the creative juices flowing when I was creating a brick walkway, strumming on my guitar, or back in my radio days, putting together a commercial combining words and background music with just the right mix, and timing it to come out exactly at sixty seconds.

Rev. LaVonne: As a professional actress I get to breath life into roles and when blessed with a creative director and an ensemble cast we have the ability to enhance one another and the audience by our collective creativity.

Dr. Don: What is creativity, anyway? Whether it's baking cookies or singing a song, creation happens when you bring your ideas to a set of pre-existing conditions and see the project transform into a manifestation of your inner vision.

Rev. LaVonne: Quoting Albert Einstein, "Creativity is seeing what everyone else has seen, and thinking what no one else has thought."

Dr. Don: The story of Jesus turning water into wine symbolizes the creative abilities of the Christ-like nature that is within you and everyone. We share this spiritual talent that God shows us because we duplicate the nature of Spirit.

Rev. LaVonne: "Each of us is an outlet to God and an inlet to God." (Ernest Holmes) When I remember that, my ideas flow and it relieves pressure since I know that Spirit is in actuality expressing the gift of creativity through me. You too are blessed with innumerable God gifts.

Dr. Don: You're in charge of how your creativity shows up in the outer world. Your conscious mind determines what the law of cause and effect will create, whether it be positive or negative. As the old-time song says, "Accentuate the positive, eliminate the negative."

Rev. LaVonne: When we all focus on the highest and best for everybody in any area of life, the result is a world that works for everyone. Imagine abundance and plenty, wellness and serenity for all people. You are a key member of a peace-filled, prosperous, healthy consciousness for the whole planet and beyond.

Dr. Don: And when you add a big dose of love to the mix, change can happen in an instant.

Rev. LaVonne: Go ahead, add Santa too and enjoy your creative Spiritual (S)"elf"!

Both: And so it is.

Divine Dialogue #51
The Gift of Joy

Rev. LaVonne: Can you imagine living a contented joyful life every day? According to the Buddha, "We are shaped by our thoughts; we become what we think. When the mind is pure, joy follows like a shadow that never leaves."

Dr. Don: I imagine Spirit expresses great joy and wants to experience it through you.

Rev. LaVonne: A good way to notice inner joy is to watch little children at play. I recently saw a young mother and her small daughter in an elegant restaurant. The child was about seven and had a doll with her. The care and loving she gave the doll told me a lot about her own parenting. It was delightful to watch the interaction between the two and see the mom playing along, discussing the doll's pretend diet with her little girl.

Dr. Don: What would bring you joy? A surge of energy or feeling aliveness and physical wellness? A mutually fulfilling romantic relationship? Experiencing the pleasure of being around children at play? Getting a raise at work or attracting financial well-being beyond your previous expectations?

Rev. LaVonne: Do you know that all these joy-filled ideas are possible to manifest? When you are in alignment with your inner Source, your Spirit-self attracts all this and more. How do I know that? Because, I believe when you have any idea, the idea comes from Spirit and dwells within. Spirit wants to be expressed through everyone.

Dr. Don: Joy can bring a smile, a laugh or if you feel it fully, tears may flow. We recently saw a Disney movie that precipitated all these reactions. The happiest place on Earth can actually exist right where you are.

Rev. LaVonne: We usually write our column in a coffee shop. It's fun to feel the energy of the happy people seeking a relaxing environment. Today, I looked up and saw a sign that read: "We tend to seek happiness when happiness is actually a choice." Good point.

Dr. Don: One of the employees apparently hadn't connected to the sign, or perhaps had made other choices omitting joy in the job that day. I sent her love and light and watched her smile.

Rev. LaVonne: A baby awoke from her nap and began to cry. The mother's comforting love brought the baby back to her natural state of happiness. Ultimately, feeling loved and being loving is tantamount to joy.

Dr. Don: The baby got over it right away. You can too. Give up the grudge.

Rev. LaVonne: "Your success and happiness lies in you. Resolve to keep happy, and your joy and you shall form an invincible host against difficulties." (Helen Keller)

Dr. Don: Finding the joy in life is contagious. Give it away, spread your joy and resolve to maintain happiness. Adopt an attitude of gratitude and let the good times roll! It's a wonderful life after all.

Both: And so it is.

Divine Dialogue #52
Expect the Best

Dr. Don: You don't have to be a fortuneteller to predict your future. What do you expect to happen? Whatever you are holding in your mind tends to take form in the outer world. The word *expect* actually means "to look forward to" or "an occurrence that is probable, likely or certain."

Rev. LaVonne: I recently spent time with a longtime friend from many miles away. The first half of our lunch was listening to him recite the myriad of problems in his life. One after the other they spewed forth. It was exhausting to take it in, so I had to counter his victim-hood with positive thoughts and occasionally lighten up the mood with a jibe or joke. It worked.

Dr. Don: It is not uncommon for people to expect the worst in life. We are barraged by news stories that tend to focus on the bad and how awful things could be.

Rev. LaVonne: Maybe some people like to struggle.

Dr. Don: Or is it a law of inertia that states that a body set in motion will stay in motion until met with an equal and opposing force? If things have always been negative, that tendency will continue until stopped.

Rev. LaVonne: And, a positive idea or force also perpetuates itself until met with an equal force in the other direction.

Dr. Don: For example, if I have a belief that money is scarce or hard to get, I'll experience lack and limitation. The experience of financial hard times will continue until I change my thinking by affirming, something like, "I am prosperous. I know the abundance that God provides is mine right now."

Rev. LaVonne: So, expect the best. Ernest Holmes wrote in the book, *This Thing Called You*, "Expectancy speeds progress. Therefore, live in a continual state of expectancy. No matter how much good you are experiencing today, expect greater good tomorrow."

Dr. Don: It's important to understand how unfulfilled expectations can lead to upset. The next time you find yourself getting angry, sad or unhappy, ask yourself "What was I expecting that didn't come about?"

Rev. LaVonne: There's an old song that starts: "Afraid it won't come 'round again, afraid to move on..." If that describes you, then here's an easy and instant solution. Put God in the center of yourself, your life, and your situations and experience the change.

Dr. Don: If you desire in the New Year to have greater peace, love, prosperity, healing or a deeper spiritual understanding, you can set your expectations in motion through prayer. "If we ask anything according to his will he hears us...We are assured that we have already received from him those things that we desire." (I John 5:14-15)

Rev. LaVonne: Why not set into motion your innermost desires, right this minute. Take a moment, close your eyes, relax and envision your perfect life. Go ahead, have a wonderful and joyous New Year as you expect the best.

Both: And so it is.

About the Authors
Rev. LaVonne Rae Andrews/Welsh
and Dr. Don Welsh

Rev. LaVonne and Dr. Don married in 2006, having been ministerial colleagues for about five years and acquaintances since 1989. Their paths just missed crossing many times in between.

Rev. LaVonne's first newspaper was *The Beach Drive Gazette* when she was eleven years old. In it she announced her big sister's engagement and sold the paper for five cents to a neighbor who had his eyes on sis – oops! Years later, on the heels of her amateur acting career, Rev. LaVonne wrote theatre reviews for *The Coasting,* an entertainment guide in Carmel, California. She also wrote a review for *The Salinas Californian* and had a monthly column "Stage Whispers" in *The Call Board* for the Monterey Theatre Alliance.

While living in Los Angeles, pursuing a professional acting career, she attended the North Hollywood Church of Religious Science under the leadership of Rev. Dr. Mark Vierra. While there, she became a Religious Science Practitioner, went on to receive her Masters Degree at the Holmes Institute, then located at the Agape Center of Truth headed by Rev. Dr. Michael Bernard Beckwith.

After finishing her two-year internship, she became ordained in 2007. Presently, Rev. LaVonne serves as Co-Minister with her husband, Dr. Don Welsh at the Central Coast Center for Spiritual Living in Templeton, California.

Inspiration for creating this book came from Steven King's book, *On Writing,* which infused new energy in the couple's weekly column in *The Paso Robles Press.*

Her advice? "Allow your inner child to shine. Smile and love the journey. Blessings and love."

Dr. Don spent 23 years in broadcasting as an announcer and personality DJ. He studied Unity and Science of Mind teachings as early as 1968 and began his ministry in Ventura, California in 1989, moving to Miami, Florida; Lancaster, California and together with Rev. LaVonne, the Central Coast Center for Spiritual Living in Templeton, California, beginning in 2009.

In the mid-1990's, he received a vision from Spirit to take up writing. It took him until 2014 to publish his first book, *The Mystical 10* immediately followed by *New Thought Genesis.*

Their next book is a comparison of Native American spirituality and the New Thought philosophy, *The Sacred Quest.* That was the topic of workshops the "Rovin' Revs" presented in many parts of the country when they traveled in their motor home as *Spirit on Wheels.* This fulfilled guidance Rev. LaVonne had received while visioning during her ministerial schooling.

As always, they will tune in to Divine Inspiration and write what's right!

Rev. LaVonne and Dr. Don may be contacted at the Center for Spiritual Living, 689 Crocker St., Templeton, CA 93456. (805) 434-9447.
www.centerforspiritualliving.org
donwelsh@sbcglobal.net
revlavonne@sbcglobal.net

Rev. LaVonne Rae Andrew/Welsh and Dr. Don Welsh

www.ingramcontent.com/pod-product-compliance
Lightning Source LLC
Chambersburg PA
CBHW061832040426
42447CB00012B/2926